PUERTO RICO
1965-1990

A Quarter Century of Highlights,
Hope, Status and Stasis

Robert Friedman

PUERTO RICO
1965-1990

*A Quarter Century of Highlights,
Hope, Status and Stasis*

A Personal History

Charleston, SC
www.PalmettoPublishing.com

PUERTO RICO; 1965-1990 A Quarter Century of Highlights,
Hope, Status and Stasis

Copyright © 2022 by Robert Friedman

First Edition

Paperback ISBN: 978-1-68515-282-6
eBook ISBN: 978-1-68515-283-3

Table of Contents

To Oscar "Ozzie"--
So he will know about the past.

To Maddy, Lizzy and Mike--
So they will remember the way it was.

Introduction

I have tried in these pages to show, through my newspaper articles and recollections of the time, what it was like
living in Puerto Rico from the mid-1960s through the 1970s
and 1980s. Those were the years I spent on the island as a
journalist for the *San Juan Star*. I also freelanced in those
years as special correspondent for the *Daily News*. The stories for the New York newspaper begin with the San Juan
dateline (minus the date). The dates when the articles were
published are at the end of the stories. The stories published
later, after I became the *Star's* Washington correspondent in
1991, relate to events that had been developing while I was
in Puerto Rico. I've also done some editing of the original
stories for clarity. This is far from an encompassing history,
more of a personal one.

My first impressions of the island and its people came
from two principal sources: the film version of *West Side
Story* and the year I spent as an investigator for the New
York City Department of Welfare. These, admittedly, were
not very impressive sources to understand much about
Puerto Rico and Puerto Ricans. Still, through my work at the
Welfare Department, I learned some things about my Puerto
Rican "clients." What struck me was their fundamental

decency in the tough struggle to survive in the oft-times nightmarish (for them) New York in order to pursue the American Dream.

I went on vacation to the island in 1964 and while there got an appointment to meet with the managing editor of the five-year-old *San Juan Star*. The newspaper already had won a Pulitzer Prize (in 1961), for editorials criticizing the island's Catholic bishops for attempting to unduly influence the election against Gov. Luis Muñoz Marín. Among other things, the governor backed a birth control program for the island. At my meeting with Managing Editor Andy Viglucci I was told something might be coming up soon. A few months later I was hired as a copy editor on the news desk. Soon after, I became a reporter.

When I settled in at the *Star* and in my new home-away-from-home in Old San Juan, I was as ignorant as most statesiders about the life, history, culture and the hard and colorful times of the people and the place. Why were so many Puerto Ricans on this lovely island concerned about an "identity crisis"? Sure, there were Burger Kings and Kentucky Fried Chicken franchises all over the place, and then, as now, the island was in political limbo. But my early impression was that Puerto Ricans knew "*a fondo*" who they were and what they valued and believed in.

One of the first stories I wrote for the *Star* happened to be an interview in 1965 with one of the creators of the Broadway show that led to the image that many statesiders, and others, had about Puerto Ricans. I interviewed Leonard Bernstein, who wrote the gorgeous music for *West Side Story*, the play and movie that gave many people their first, and for a long time, only reference about all those migrants from that U.S. territory in the Caribbean.

When I came to the island, I was somewhat surprised that a good number of the residents were put off by the Broadway and Hollywood "stereotyping" of their stateside brethren. Ironically, just one Puerto Rican had a major role in the play (Chita Rivera) and only one in the movie (Rita Moreno).

So there I was in Puerto Rico, an island known to most of the U.S. populace only as the original home of the Sharks, the Puerto Rican gang of *West Side Story*, interviewing one of the show's creators, who was on the island to conduct the orchestra of one of the world's most prestigious musical gatherings, the Casals Festival. The festival was named after one of the world's most prestigious musicians, the cellist Pablo Casals. The Spanish musician had been living in Puerto Rico since 1956, in self-imposed exile from the dictatorship of Francisco Franco.

The Bernstein interview took place in his room at the Caribe Hilton Hotel. Bernstein was relaxed in a robe and smoking cigarettes and was warm and friendly. When I asked him about the film version of *West Side Story*, he said the original Broadway production was better and he was critical of some of the casting in the movie, but asked me not to write about his comparisons. Which I didn't.

A few days after I interviewed Bernstein, I saw him at the Tapia Theater in Old San Juan, enjoying a production of *Who's Afraid of Virginia Woolf?*, staged by a local English-language theater group. I figured that there must be more to this small, 100-by-35-mile home to some 3 million sort-of U.S. citizens (minus certain rights, like voting representation in Congress and casting ballots for president) than meets the average American eye.

That was then, and I imagine still is, now.

Bernstein Tells of Genesis of West Side Story Theme

Great works of art burn with universal truths for all time; the spark, which 'fires up' the artist's imagination, usually ignites from his or her own time.

Such was the case with *West Side Story,* according to Leonard Bernstein, world-famous conductor, composer, and performer, who wrote the music for the world-traveled, highly honored musical drama.

Bernstein, who is here to perform tonight at the Casals Festival, said in an interview Saturday at the Caribbean Hilton Hotel that the idea for the modern theme of *West Side Story* had been with him several years. But it didn't "catch fire" until 1955—"when a new racial problem became evident." He was referring to the hostilities, harassments, and heartaches faced by many Puerto Ricans in the time of their greatest exodus to the mainland

Bernstein explained that the original idea was to set the action on New York's Lower East Side involving Jewish and Italian gangs.

"But this idea lacked interest. It was outdated," the sharply featured conductor of the New York Philharmonic Symphony Orchestra said. "Years later, the time arrived and fired our imagination," he said,

"I suppose this was part of a negative inspiration, like saying that if Puerto Ricans didn't have to face these problems, the play would not have been written," Bernstein said.

"I would rather that these problems didn't exist and not have written the show," he added.

Asked if he plans to compose another musical, the 48-eight-year-old, multi-talented musician replied, rather sadly, that he had recently abandoned a musical version of Thornton Wilder's *The Skin of Our Teeth.*

"I worked for six months on the play, but unfortunately, it collapsed. It was heart-breaking."

However, he said that he has just completed a composition for an English cathedral— a set of psalms, written in Hebrew. He said that composing the psalms was "a sort of critical moment" for him as a composer.

"I was trying to decide whether I was going to write something avant-garde or old-fashioned, whether I was going to be in or out. I decided to compose pretty old-fashioned music."

Bernstein, whose musical interests are broad, commented on recent attempts to elevate rock- and-roll to a musical pop art form. "I think the only way this type of music can enter into an art form," he said, "is through the theatre. It can be used to comment on itself. I'm very fond of the Beatles, but I don't think they think of themselves as artists."

He said music was experiencing a very peculiar moment. Everyone is searching, but nothing outstanding has yet been offered.

"Part of the trouble is that the symphonic form, which realized its logical historical climax with Mahler, seems to have been in decline ever since. Composers today are not really writing symphonies.

"If this is true, then the symphonic orchestra, which is the externalization of the symphonic form, is becoming a kind of museum, and the conductor," he added wistfully, "is becoming the museum's curator."

June 2, 1965

Leonard Bernstein

Home Away from Home

*F*or the expats, it was Greenwich Village South. For the nouveau well-to-do, it was a chance to gentrify in their newly restored colonial homes. For the majority of others, it was a living, vibrant community where life had a distinctive style, high and low, where rich and poor lived side-by-side in pastel-colored houses and where cultural activities abounded.

Where the painters, poets, pugilists, laborers, lawyers, storekeepers, students, unemployed and uninhibited spent their days and nights mostly walking (few residents drove) along the blue cobblestone streets, in and out of the many bars and restaurants and artist haunts, in the hilly seven-block-square area. The streets opened to tree-shaded plazas and closed with views of the ocean above and the bay below. There were museums and schools and newly restored homes and old Spanish fortresses and very old city walls and, especially for the tourists, jewelry shops and schlocky souvenir stores. There were also the homeless sleeping in doorways and junkies nodding on street corners. And late, late night, there were scores of cats who came out to claim the silent streets and passageways. That was Old San Juan in the decades of the Sixties, Seventies and Eighties.

Much of the island art world lived in those blocks at that time, painters such as Rafael Tufiño, Manuel Hernández Acevedo, Carlos Irizarry, Domingo García; writers Emilio Díaz Valcárcel and René Marqués; Ballets de San Juan Artistic Director Ana García; Institute of Puerto Rican Culture chief Ricardo Alegría, who was the anthropologist responsible for the renovation and restoration of the Old City. There were wonderful museums, such as one dedicated to the music of Pablo Casals (now located in the Santurce section of San Juan) and La Casa del Libro, where you could see how books were made and view such samples as a page of a Gutenberg Bible and lots of 15th Century books printed in Spain.

The *colmado* on the corner of Calle Cruz and Calle San Sebastián, had a sign behind the counter: "*Aquí no se habla de política*" (No talking politics here). In the plazas, fruit vendors sold oranges peeled in a machine that looked like a vise, the skin curling off like paper streamers. Domino players slapped tiles on cement tables; horse players sat along a wall with pink racing forms in their laps, figuring their fortunes for the day.

One of my favorite places for a refreshing drink was *La Vida en Broma* (Life as a Joke), where you could get a juicy glass of *tamarindo*, *guanábana* or *ajonjolí*. You could also buy single cigarettes there or a shot of rum in a paper cup. And, of course, many breakfasts were consumed at La Bombonera, the *café con leche* and *mallorca* capital of the hemisphere. Behind the counter was a wonderful decades-old big shiny silver Cuban coffee-making machine giving off steam from its valves and tubes. The servers, all male, seldom smiled, but were quick and efficient. Sotomayor, whose face was creased from forehead to chin and whose quips hit the sarcastic spot, was my favorite waiter. The back tables were always occupied by elderly gentlemen in *guayaberas* and Panama hats who took apart the latest political move by whoever was in charge at the time. After operating for 110 years, the restaurant shut down in 2012.

On Calle San Sebastián, El Patio de Sam was, and still is, located across from the statue of Juan Ponce de León, whose remains are just down the street in the San Juan Cathedral. On Cristo and Fortaleza Street, the now-shuttered Ocho Puertas featured some of the island's most famous singers— Lucecita Benítez, Danny Rivera, Chucho Avellanet, et. al., and singer-songwriter-satirist Raoul González, who defined himself as a "*Borinquen Yanqui*, bilingual, bicultural, *Bei Mir Bist Du Schoen* and Babalú."

There were kite-flying weekends when hundreds of kids and their parents ran and tugged strings across the huge grassy lawn of El Morro fortress to fly beautifully and awkwardly homemade kites, along with the store-bought models, and saw their creations climb up, up in the air and sometimes come crashing down into the historic Old City walls around the fortress.

The Colibrí Gallery on Cristo Street, presided over by art lover-dealer-collector Luigi Marrozzini, had many exhibits of works by local artists and some rather notable others, like Ben Shahn and Pablo Picasso.

The following article of a walking tour I took of Old San Juan one day in 1984 noted the good, the bad, the ugly and the beautiful.

Old City—Ancient, Decadent, Priceless

Walking tour of Old San Juan: Where beauty and seediness coexist, complement one another. Where restored, 18th Century, pastel-colored houses slope steeply toward the bay and rise above the ocean. Where gleaming white ships circle the city, and Cristopher Columbus, holding a Spanish flag, oversees all on a high white pedestal.

Carbon monoxide fills the air in Plaza Colón. It comes from the line of buses that keep their motors running while drivers take half-hour coffee breaks. Passengers sit on the low wall surrounding the plaza, looking as though they have all the time in the world, as they wait for a bus to move into action.

Heavy-leaved trees gather in the cool in the Old City's other plazas and a one-legged tramp sleeps on the sidewalk, in the middle of San Francisco Street, his head against the padded armrests of his crutches.

Up past La Barandilla, on the low wall that slopes along Tanca Street, seating space is at a minimum. Old men rest there, staring down the day. The horse players hold transistors to their ears, yellow scratch sheets laid out beside them. I remember often seeing junkies leaning at the corner of Tanca and Luna at dizzying 45-degree angles. Today, the corner is drug-free.

Luna Street—once filled almost nightly with sailors spinning groggily from hooker bar to hooker bar, before it was taken over by bouffant-haired blondes in Carmen Miranda shoes and with two-day beard growths—is now up for sale. Everywhere there are signs that the Blanca Gandia Realty Company is selling Luna Street, building by building.

Lunch at the Acropolis on Tanca Street, one of the few Puerto Rican-Greek restaurants in captivity. The feta omelette (Greek goat cheese) is a treat.

On Cristo Street, Ricardo Alegría, the director of the Institute of Puerto Rican Culture and the man responsible for the lovely restoration of the Old City, talks of Regulation 5, which prohibits signs from jutting into the street. We look up and down Cristo. Signs are jutting all over the place. He mentions that Regulation 5 also prohibits the changing of building facades.

Facades are being changed up and down San Francisco and Fortaleza Streets. Wherever there's a phony marble front, you can bet it's a new jewelry store.

Further up Cristo Street, El Convento, once a home for nuns, now a hotel for the discriminating (in the best sense) tourist, appears peaceful despite the never-ending traffic rolling by its side windows and doors.

Meanderings down lower Sol, which is still one of the most lovely, peaceful sections of the Old City. A flute sonata wafts on the warm, still air. I pass the house where I once lived, in a tunnel-like apartment that gave light at the end with a dramatic terrace view of the bay. I remember the girl some houses down who used to sit hours by her window, singing along with recordings by the Supremes, her voice a match for Diana Ross'.

Up the steps of the plant-filled Caleta del Hospital, down to Casa Blanca. The gardens back there used to be a favorite reading and relaxation spot. It is still cool and shady, but the fountain no longer gurgles, the landscaping is overgrown with weeds, hammers pound and

drills screech from a nearby restoration going on.

I move back towards the heart of the Old City, pass the locations of the noted and notorious bars of the past. El Batey is still on Cristo Street in all its bombed-out garage splendor. Ocho Puertas, where local talent was appreciated long before the hotels got on the bandwagon, is now . . . guess what? . . . a jewelry store. The Malamute, where the clock stopped permanently for its clientele at three o'clock in the morning of the soul, is now a beauty supplies store. The boisterous El Prado, where buxom, middle-aged, alleged prostitutes reportedly hung out, has gone dainty, converted into Le Petit Café.

I pass the Hotel Central in Plaza de Armas. The hotel has become the Old City's Little Haiti. A woman walks by with a large basket of goods on her head, just like in the old country. Haitian women shop in a bargain store next to the hotel, give directions in Franglish to men transferring large cartons from the hotel lobby onto a truck.

I move to The Bookstore on San José Street. Richard Gilpen, one of the last of a dying breed, a bookstore owner who actually cares about books, says the big seller this month is

"Apalabramiento," a collection of short stories by Puerto Rican writers, such as Luis Rafael Sánchez, Rosario Ferré and Magali García Ramis.

I meet the artist Carlos Irizarry who tells me the National Center for the Arts, across from San Francisco Church, is being restored, that classes in painting, print-making, music, dance, theater will be given there again and that he is the new administrator.

Carlos Mebs, owner of the Barranchina restaurant-jewelry store-dress shop-complex, stands disconsolately in front of his emporium, bewailing the lack of cruise ships in port. No cruise ships, says Mebs, no tourists.

Another jeweler insists that this is the worst tourism season yet.

Up to Plaza de San José, where Ponce de León, the island's first governor, stands in stone, pointing all the way down to San Juan Bay, perhaps recalling his trip to the island from Florida, either still searching for the Fountain of Youth or the plentiful deposits of gold said to be found in the local rivers and streams. Across the street from the statue of the Spanish *conquistador* is El Patio de Sam, noted bar-restaurant hangout for the island's painters, poets, politicians and pugilists.

Back down the blue brick streets of the Old City--the bricks once used as ballast for

Christopher Columbus stands tall in the plaza that bears his name at the entrance to Old San Juan

the Spanish Armada, and other vessels--to the small park at the foot of San José Street. The park overlooks the onetime notorious La Princesa Jail, where families and sweethearts used to stand on the edge of the wall conversing with their loved ones who looked up from behind the barred windows.

The seedy sight gives way to splendor with a panoramic view of the harbor. Tall palms fringe the shore, boats glide by. The furthest hills beyond Cataño look like blue traces of the ones in the foreground. The bay sparkles like it is filled with diamonds.

Like diamonds, Old San Juan is forever.

Jan. 27, 1984

Trumpeter Dale Wales, a stalwart of the Puerto Rico jazz scene in the 1960s – 1980s, plays his horn on a midnight street in Old San Juan, (Photo by Marvin W. Schwartz)

The Diaspora

*I*t was a record-breaking exodus for the time, called the Great Migration, when between the years 1950-1960, a reported 470,000 Puerto Ricans left the island, moving to the states, mostly to New York and the East Coast. The Commonwealth government of the time was far from disappointed at the island's population loss; its leaders were seen as encouraging it. Many of those who left for the states were the displaced poor of the countryside; having them leave the island allowed the government to concentrate on its Operation Bootstrap economic program that brought manufacturing plants down from the states. The program gave the manufacturers a tax haven and they employed hundreds of thousands of island residents in their labor-intensive factories; a Puerto Rican middle-class was created.

Though the late 1960s saw a relatively healthy island economy, local farming, long a mainstay, practically disappeared, falling to less than one percent of the island's economic output and placing a very high reliance on imported food. In the burgeoning island supermarkets were oranges from California, bananas from the Dominican Republic, avocados from Mexico. Imports also included such staples as rice and beans and coffee. Since the Jones Act of 1917 requires all imports be brought to the island on expensive American ships, prices were far more expensive in a Puerto Rico Pueblo supermarket than in a stateside Safeway.

Before the Great Migration, more modest Puerto Rican settlements in New York occurred from about 1917 until the end of World War II. During those years, the Puerto Rican "exiles," many of whom were skilled workers such as cigar makers, integrated into neighborhoods with Cubans and Spaniards. There were no reports at the time of *West Side Story* gangs or social diseases among the populace.

In the post-war years, Puerto Rican communities grew and grew, expanding into *El Barrio* in East Harlem, the South Bronx and Williamsburg in Brooklyn. The migrants already had three strikes against them: they were unskilled workers with little education and not much English. The one-time island residents and their brethren grew into the second largest minority in the city after Blacks, the second-largest Latin population on the mainland after Mexicans and, along with Native Americans, among the most economically disadvantaged minority groups.

Then, when the economy got really dicey for them, both in the states and on the island, came the revolving door and the reverse migration of the 1970s and 1980s. More than 250,000 *Boricuas* returned to the island of their own or their forefathers' birth. A lot of the "Neoricans" or *"Nuyoricans"* had problems adjusting to their homeland. The "Neoricans" vented their feelings in the following story.

(The island's recent economic problems has caused another massive migration, mostly to Florida, in the Orlando and Miami areas. Only time will tell, and the rulers in

Washington will determine, whether another reverse migration will occur sometime in the future—if and when the island's economy ever recovers.)

Neoricans—Unwelcome in 2 Worlds

SAN JUAN, P.R.—For the Neo Ricans of Puerto Rico, rejection and discrimination have not ended on their return home.

Puerto Ricans who were born or raised in the United States are returning in ever-increasing numbers to the island most consider their true homeland. But many of them are confronting problems and prejudices they thought they were putting behind when they stepped off the jets from up north into the warm tropical breezes of *La Isla*.

Because most of the returnees come from the New York area, they are called by island-born residents Neuyoricans, or Neoricans, usually pejorative terms meaning loud, pushy, uncultured. And because they speak a Spanish that is strongly accented or limited, they are considered *Americanos*, meaning they are foreigners, not true Puerto Ricans.

Many come back to Puerto Rico looking for their roots. Often they are met with disdain and discrimination by their countrymen.

"It's a weird scene," said Julio Machado, who moved to Puerto Rico a year ago with his wife and three children. "In New York, people will call you a spik. In Puerto Rico, you open your mouth and speak English, they put you down by calling you an *Americano*."

Others have recently migrated back to the island because of New York's financial woes. But the search for even the most menial job here has often turned into a discouraging and frustrating experience.

Anna Byron Rodríguez worked as a front office cashier for the Commodore Hotel on E. 42d St., until it closed down a year ago last May. For the past six months, she has searched fruitlessly for a job in Puerto Rico.

"At first," she said, "I had it in mind to work at one of the big tourist hotels. I couldn't find anything. Then I tried the department stores, asking if they needed a cashier. Nothing. I've been all over, filling out forms, being interviewed. I recently went to a little store that sells beer and soda and potato chips.

11

I had to wait three hours with three other girls until the boss arrived. He interviewed for 15 minutes in a dumpy office in the back, then said he'll call me if he wants me. The job is for Saturdays and Sundays, $15 a day. I used to make $150 a week in New York.

"But by now, I'll take anything. I'm used to working. Doing nothing is driving me crazy."

Byron added: "When I was in New York, so many people who had just come back from Puerto Rico told me, 'There's nothing down there in the way of jobs.' But I didn't believe them. I had to go see for myself. Now I'm very disappointed."

The Commonwealth Labor Department's unemployment figure for the island is 20%. But even government officials admit that the real figure, counting those who have dropped out of the job market, is closer to double that, which is much worse than the worst years of the Great Depression in the United States. Unemployment benefits are available, and more than 60% of families receive food stamps. But other aid is practically nonexistent. A welfare recipient in Puerto Rico gets between $14 and $18 a month.

Puerto Rico has been hit very hard in the past few years by both recession and inflation—and this has happened at a time when migration patterns have reversed. Many more Puerto Ricans are arriving than are leaving for the states. Some 40,000 Puerto Ricans, whether returning migrants or U.S.-born, arrived here in fiscal 1976. There are an estimated 250,000 to 300,000 Puerto Ricans born or reared on the mainland who are now living on this island of 3.2 million inhabitants. Of these returnees, about 60,000 are school-age children who do not know enough Spanish to follow classroom work. Unlike New York, where bilingual programs are required for Spanish-speaking schoolchildren, the Education Department in Puerto Rico has no bilingual program, although plans call for such a program at seven schools in January.

In the 1950s and 60s, Puerto Rico made great economic and social strides under its Operation Bootstrap industrialization program. Between 1952 and 1971, however, almost 600,000 Puerto Ricans were leaving the island, a mass migration which, some observers feel, was spurred by the government to ease the population and unemployment problems. Those who migrated were mostly untouched by Puerto Rico's economic "miracle." They went looking for a better life in the states.

For many, America did not prove to be the promised-land. They, and their sons and daughters, are now returning to the island to find that their search has not yet ended. They are caught between two cultures: in their hearts, they are Puerto Rican; in their habits, mostly American. And they feel accepted by neither.

"Those of us who went up to the states found discrimination because of the language barrier," said Frank Mirabel. "For those who were born up there and came down here it's been the same—the language barrier and discrimination. You're a stranger up there and you're a stranger down here. Where do you belong?"

Mirabel, who settled in Puerto Rico six years ago after being born and raised in Manhattan, is still asking himself that question. Currently employed as a banquet and sales representative for a San Juan tourist hotel, he exudes at first the sense of a go-getter who has little time to fret over identity. But as the conversation continues, he expresses strong feelings about the rejection he has experienced.

"You feel Puerto Rican all your life. So you want to come back to your roots. And one day you do and then you get hit with all this. They tell you you're not really a Puerto Rican, just like they let you know up there that you weren't really an American. But you feel more abused here than in the states. There, in a way, you can understand it. Discrimination is worldwide. But why with your own? Why can't you be accepted? Your roots and your family are here."

The picture is not bleak for all returning Puerto Ricans. Many have adjusted more easily to the ways of the "locals" and have, in turn, been accepted to a greater degree into the mainstream of Puerto Rican life. A number of New Yoricans have become prominent in business, the professions, the arts and government. And a group of these successful returnees has formed a new organization called New Yoricans in Puerto Rico Inc. The organization will try to help the new influx of migrants get jobs and deal with the problems of unexpectedly being strangers in what they thought would be a welcoming land.

"We're going to try to create a more positive image for New Yoricans here," said Antonio Torres, the president, a computer school executive, who came to Puerto Rico from New York ten months ago. "We want to try to bring together the Puerto Ricans from New York and those who were born on the island. Even though it's warm down here, too many of us have been out in the cold too long."

Oct. 16, 1972

Status, Politics, Politicians

*P*olitics and status filled the days and nights in Puerto Rico in the mid-to-late Sixties, Seventies and Eighties—and, undoubtedly, the following decades into the 21st Century. After many years of pro-Commonwealth Popular Democratic Party rule, the statehood movement was born again in 1968 with the election of Luis A. Ferré as governor. The industrialist-newspaper publisher-patron of the arts had lost the previous two gubernatorial races—to four-term Gov. Luis Muñoz Marín in 1960 and to Roberto Sánchez Vilella in 1964. Ferré was elected this time after a split in the PDP. Sánchez Vilella, the island's second elected governor, had been drummed out of the party leadership, allegedly for moving away from the PDP's push for more industrialization on the island. The then-governor's private life didn't help his standing among the party's bigwigs either; he divorced his wife of 30 years in mid-term to marry his Fortaleza aide, Jeanette Ramos, in 1967. The "scandal" scandalized mostly members of the island's Catholic upper-class; and it was the talk of most of the island's towns at the time. Sánchez Vilella formed the People's Party to run an unsuccessful reelection campaign.

The then-governor believed that U.S. Navy officials, who had considerable clout on the island at the time, helped Ferré in his gubernatorial campaign with logistics, money and a smear campaign against him (Sánchez). Navy officials had been scorned by Sánchez as long-time meddlers in Puerto Rican affairs. During his term in office, he had cut off a telephone hotline that linked the governor's office and the local Navy command.

For what it is or isn't worth, when I interviewed Sánchez several years after he left politics, the bookcase in his office was stacked with novels of intrigue—spy books by the likes of John Le Carré, Eric Ambler, Len Deighton and Frederick Forsyth.

Although Ferré and the New Progressive Party he organized in 1967 brought new life to the statehood movement, most island voters still favored the Commonwealth relationship. In a 1967 plebiscite, the only status vote held in the years leading up to the 1990s, Commonwealth won 60 percent of the vote, statehood 37 percent and independence just 3 percent. (The Puerto Rico Independence Party boycotted the vote.) Ferré formed the NPP after the Statehood Republican Party, which until then was the party of supporters of union with the U.S., decided to boycott the plebiscite, supposedly because the results would not bind the U.S. Congress to act.

Whatever the status preference of the voters, the governorship switched back and forth during the next two decades, between PDP Gov. Rafael Hernández Colón (1973-77, 1985-89) and NPP Gov. Carlos Romero Barceló (1977-81, 1981-85). In a seemingly never-ending election spiral Hernández Colón was reelected in 1989, serving until 1993. It should be mentioned that in those years 79 percent of eligible voters cast ballots in island elections. (The mainland rate was, and still is, around 50 percent.)

Under Romero's governorship, there was lots of fiery talk, but little real action for moving Puerto Rico toward statehood. The police killings of two young *independentistas* at Cerro Maravilla in 1978 and the subsequent cover-up seriously damaged the reputation of his administration.

Hernández Colón's efforts through his New Thesis to get more power from Washington for the Commonwealth also got mostly nowhere. During his administrations, Washington shot down, among other proposals, limiting federal laws only to those that specifically mentioned the island, allowing the island to set its own minimum wage, giving the local government control over sea transportation, and the right to issue passports. Commonwealth proposals for a resident commissioner in the U.S. Senate—the island had and still has a nonvoting resident commissioner in the House—and full funding in all federal programs also got nowhere. Puerto Rico's share of federal funds is capped or non-existent in such programs as Medicaid, Medicare, Nutritional Aid, Earned Income Tax Credit and Supplemental Security Income.

(Again, apropos of not much, in interviews with the two governors, I found Hernández Colón full of facts and coolly dismissive of opinions other than his own, and Romero warm and friendly—as long as you did not beg to differ.)

In a lengthy 1984 article about Puerto Rico in *The New York Times* magazine, an island lawyer was quoted making this "gloomy" prediction: "Come back in the year 2000; we'll still be arguing about it (status)." The lawyer undoubtedly could have added several more decades to the ongoing debate.

Then there was, and still is, the island's oldest movement for a status change, which dates back to uprisings against Spanish colonial rule in the 1820s. While political independence for the island was solidly defeated in island status plebiscites, it was favored in the 1965-1989 period by many of the island's intellectuals and artists. A strong argument against that status at the time was that independence would mean the loss of U.S. citizenship, along with the accompanying ease of moving back and forth from the island to the states. Most island residents really did not want to break their links with the U.S. Nevertheless, as the saying went at the time, about midnight, when inhibitions are lifted, many Puerto Ricans, in their hearts and souls, become *independentistas*. And, at all times of the day, the majority, whether backing statehood or continued Commonwealth, supported a cultural independence for the island.

The following article, published in 1976, gives the status view of the young Puerto Rican Independence Party President Rubén Ángel Berríos.

Late governors Carlos Romero Barceló, left, and Rafael Hernández Colón greet each other with a handshake in a rare friendly moment. (José Ismael Fernández/Archivo Historico *El Nuevo Dia*)

Rubén Berríos: the Man, the Image, the Philosophy

He's "soft" on America, "hard" on abortion, pro-middle class, anti-prolonged doles to the poor, a defender of the bourgeois principle of liberal democracy, an opponent of hard-lining Marxist-Leninist authoritarianism. Some say he's the new, but he says he's the same old Rubén Berríos. The only difference, he insists, is that now a sizeable number of people in Puerto Rico are really listening to him and looking to him and his Puerto Rican Independence Party to lift the island from the morass it is rapidly sinking into.

Yes, Rubén Berríos says, he and his party are definitely in the running in 1976 and will no longer be also-rans at the polls. While still undecided whether he should run for governor or seek to renew his Senate seat, the PIP president claims that come November "something astonishing is going to happen."

What will astound, according to Berríos, is that neither the Popular Democratic Party nor the New Progressive Party will draw as much as 40 per cent of the vote and after election day

Puerto Rico "will have three minority parties and a large mixed vote. "That," said the senator, "is a brand-new ball game."

A recent PIP-conducted poll showed Berríos garnering over 15 per cent of the vote if he runs for governor and dragging along on his coattails several PIP legislators. (In 1972 the party drew 52,070 votes, a measly 4.7 per cent of the total, but Berríos collected 94,570 votes for the Senate.) The PIP leader insists, however, that if he does go for the governorship, and loses, he will not replace any party member who might gain a Senate seat in November.

Although party-conducted polls are notoriously self-serving, Berríos insists, and several local political observers agree, that the PIP, and their leader, have begun to tap roots within the Puerto Rican psyche. Something is very wrong with our society, most Puerto Ricans are saying, and Berríos is offering his diagnosis and prescription for cure and many are listening. Whether the listeners become hundreds of thousands of PIP voters in November remains to be counted.

But the image of Rubén Berríos as responsible and responsive political leader has certainly been upgraded during his Senate years. Berríos, 36, says he has always been the same man with the same qualities and that the changing times have brought more people around to paying serious attention to what he has been saying all along. Others say he has been making a conscious effort to broaden his appeal by softening his militancy. Whichever, the political truth of the matter is that others are starting to see Berríos in a more favorable light. And how one is perceived, goes a long way to how one perceives oneself.

Other things, naturally, come into play in the making of the image of the man. TV has seldom been kind to Rubén Berríos. During press conferences, on panel shows, face-to-face before the country he has, in this reporter's opinion, almost always come on too strong. His eyebrows lowering to hood his blue eyes, his features seeming to sharpen on camera, he has almost always been on the attack, Rubén the Hawk baring down on his prey. And though he almost always

seems to make the kill, sometimes you feel for the victim.

On one such show back before the 1972 elections Berríos and Roberto Sánchez Vilella were being quizzed by a panel of journalists. Berríos came on like a man possessed with the cold fire of self-righteous truth, not unlike a Plaza Colón preacher for Christ; Sánchez like a vulnerable human being who had erred in the past and had learned from his mistakes. Berríos was analyzing, proselytizing and mesmerizing; Sánchez was humanizing. And, as lots of people know, for a politician, it's not what you say on TV that leaves 'em voting, but the way you're projecting. It seemed in those days that Berríos was living up to the image of himself whipped up by the media: sharp, shrewd and surly.

And while some remnants of this image may remain whenever he appears on TV today, one can't help feeling after a two-hour face-to-face interview with the new—or the same old—real Rubén Berríos that the TV image has been too harsh. Berríos comes across in person with considerably more warmth and charm than on the tube.

But charm, warmth and image aside, Rubén Berríos is still dedicated to "deep fundamental changes in the economic, political and social structures" of the island. Meaning he is still adamant in his belief that only a combination of socialism and independence will bring "human wellbeing" to the vast majority of Puerto Ricans. And like other inseparable pairings, you can't have one, Berríos says, without the other.

"If the United States became socialist, we'd still want independence," the PIP president said.

Why? Because even socialist nations, practice economic Colonialism. Like, for instance, the Soviet Union re: the nations of Eastern Europe.

"The whole theoretical basis of the internationalism of socialism has been outgrown by reality," Berríos said. "We believe that nowadays national sovereignty is absolutely necessary, particularly for small nations, as a defense mechanism against the larger powers."

In fact, the whole idea of what socialism is, or could be, has to be rethought, according to Berríos. And Puerto Rico has become one of the testing grounds for the rethinking, the senator believes.

"Socialism is the wave of the future, that I'm sure of," he said. "And the struggle of the future—in the United States, as well as in Russia—will be between democratic socialism and authoritarian socialism."

This struggle is being played out in today's Puerto Rico within a socialist framework through the recently widened split between the PIP and the Puerto Rican Socialist Party. Berríos says the split over "very serious ideological differences" and the two parties are as far apart "as heaven and earth."

Berríos sees PIP as representing the democratic socialists, the believers in decentralization of power and decision-making for the people, the defenders of civil liberties and human rights, all of which puts that party "a long way from the authoritarian socialists and makes us (the PIP) differ radically from the PSP's classical Marxism-Leninism." And the hard-lining PSP, Berríos intimates, stands for just the opposite: a ruling bureaucracy that is neither very civil about liberties nor very human about rights.

The PSP has countered that Berríos is little more than your average reformer-within-the-system who is not really interested in revolutionary changes. Berríos shrugs off these counter-charges.

Does he consider himself a revolutionary?

"The term 'revolutionary' has been confused with rock-throwing, yelling and bomb-throwing. It started with Copernicus when he spoke about a revolution of the heavenly bodies, which altered the previously held Ptolemaic theory of astronomy. It denoted a fundamental change of what was previously accepted. And that is what I, and the PIP, stand for: deep fundamental changes."

Berríos noted that when he speaks of the opposition he does not mean the American people, per se. And he has recently said if and when the island ever became an independent nation he would want to keep good relations with the U.S., all of which proves, in some people's books, that the legislator is rapidly growing "soft" toward the U.S.

"People who say that," he retorted, "never took the care to see what the PIP and I believe, I've always said the same. It's not a matter of being soft or hard, but of making yourself respected in the world. I've always said that being anti-American is as nauseating as being anti-Chinese or anti-French or anti-any country. You can be against U.S. business in Puerto Rico, against Soviet tanks in Czechoslovakia. You don't have to be anti, just pro-Puerto Rican and against the colonialization of your land." said the legislator.

Feb 2, 1976

Rubén Berríos, Age 37, in 1976.

Death of the Titans

*T*hey were Puerto Rico's two political giants of the 20th Century. When Nationalist leader Pedro Albizu Campos passed away on April 21, 1965 at age 73, some 75,000 mourners reportedly accompanied the funeral procession for his burial in the Old San Juan cemetery. Luis Muñoz Marín died on April 30, 1980 at 82. Many tens of thousands mourned his death. After his body lay in state at the island Capitol building, he was buried in Barranquitas, the small central mountain town of his birth. The political life and the fate of the two men were inextricably tied together. In 1950, Albizu was convicted and imprisoned for planning armed uprisings that were carried out in several cities in Puerto Rico. Among the targets were La Fortaleza and the sitting governor, Muñoz Marín. Albizu suffered various illnesses in the federal prison and was pardoned by Muñoz in 1964, just a few months before his death. There is controversy over his treatment in prison. Albizu alleged that he was the subject of radiation experiments in prison and said that he could see colored rays bombarding him. When he wrapped wet towels around his head in order to shield himself from the radiation, the prison guards ridiculed him as *El Rey de las Toallas* (The King of the Towels).

Pedro Albizu Campos

(Officials suggested that Albizu was suffering from mental illness. But here are the words of an official U.S. document released in 1995 by the Advisory Committee on Human Radiation Experiments: "Committee finds that from 1944 to 1974 the government sponsored . . . several thousand human radiation experiments. These experiments were conducted by researchers affiliated with government agencies, universities, hospitals and other research institutions. The Advisory Committee finds that some of the biomedical experiments reviewed were ethically, troubling were conducted on institutionalized children, seriously ill and sometimes comatose patients, African-Americans and prisoners. It was common to conduct research on patients without their consent.")

Albizu leaves a legacy of fierce integrity, of never wavering in his beliefs and of fearlessly facing any opposition to those beliefs, no matter how powerful. Both Muñoz and Albizu started out backing independence for Puerto Rico;.While Albizu continued until his death the fight of the martyr for true political independence, Muñoz became a true politician who created a compromising political, economic and social relationship with the island's Washington overlords.

While in some island political circles Muñoz is blamed for the island's seemingly never-ending status stalemate, leading to its psycho-socio-political hang-ups and its economic hard times, he *was* elected to four terms as governor by the Puerto Rican people. He has been correctly criticized for such moves as keeping the so-called *ley de la mordaza* (gag law), aimed at shutting up and shutting down the independence movement, in effect for too many years while he was governor. Franklin Delano Roosevelt, another four-term chief executive, also made mistakes during his reign—imprisoning Japanese-Americans and giving a cold shoulder to asylum-seeking Jews during World War II trying to pack the Supreme Court with New Deal-friendly judges he knew would allow him to push his favorite laws. Roosevelt was, of course, a politician, and so was Muñoz, and by now we all know about politicians—even the best of them have to look every-which-way over every shoulder to possibly, hopefully, accomplish something. Nevertheless, any impartial observer would see that Roosevelt did more good than harm for more people in the United States, just as Muñoz did in Puerto Rico.

Luis Muñoz Marín

Thousands Bid Farewell in Steady Rotunda Stream

Thousands upon thousands of Puerto Ricans—most waiting patiently beneath a broiling sun—continued their pilgrimage to the Capital Thursday to bid a heartfelt farewell to Luis Muñoz Marín.

A steady stream of humanity poured into the island's Legislature from sunrise to darkness to view the casket holding the remains of the former governor, who died Wednesday. Officials who organized the two-day wake in the rotunda estimated at least 60,000 people will have seen the casket before it is moved at 9 a.m. today to San Juan Cathedral.

Cardinal Luis Aponte Martinez will say a requiem mass at 10 a.m. during the cathedral services. Former Resident Commissioner Jaime Benítez, a long-time associate of Muñoz, will deliver the eulogy.

The funeral cortege is scheduled to leave the cathedral at noon to wind its way to the central mountain town of Barranquitas where the Popular Democratic Party founder will be laid to rest. Former Gov. Rafael Hernández Colón will offer the graveside eulogy.

Puerto Ricans of all ages and walks of life came in from the powerful heat of the sun to find stifling heat inside the Capitol. But they appeared oblivious to the conditions as they paid homage to the man whose immense accomplishments have suddenly been resurrected in the island's collective memory by his death.

Mourners laid flowers—as well as rosaries and rings—atop the flag draping the gray metal casket, which remained closed throughout the wake. Those passing touched the casket, kissed it, blessed themselves, prayed and shed tears.

An emotional moment occurred when Ines Mendoza vda, de Muñoz, the former governor's wife, returned to the Capitol at about 4:15 p.m. She had been taken, in exhaustion, to her Trujillo Alto home by relatives in the early hours of the morning. As she entered the rotunda, several friends of

26

many years broke into tears as they rushed to embrace her.

Mrs. Muñoz went to the coffin, knelt, moved the upper half of her body back and forth, then put her head down on the casket.

Among those who paid their respects alongside the casket was Marta Casals Istomin, widow of cellist Pablo Casals, who spent the latter part of his life on the island. Muñoz had been instrumental in bringing the great Spanish musician to Puerto Rico. She said she was expressing her admiration in the name of her late husband for "all Don Luis has done for culture, music, the arts and spiritual values." She added that she was also grateful for the support Muñoz and his wife had given her and Casals.

And a hush fell in the rotunda when Rafael Muñoz z Zequeira, the 7-year-old great-grandson of the former governor, knelt before the casket to pray. The boy is the son of Rafael Muñoz Arjona, who is the son of Luis Muñoz Lee, the former governor's only son.

Earlier in the afternoon, Cardinal Aponte said a prayer in front of the bier and 35 members of the University of Puerto Rico chorus sang sacred choral works, their voices ringing clearly though the high domed hall.

As the day progressed, many more floral wreaths were delivered and placed against walls to offer a colorful background to a wake that was at the same time sorrowful in its mourning and joyful in its memories of Muñoz.

Among those who made the pilgrimage to pay homage to the creator of Commonwealth were Aurea Ayala, 67, and Fernina Lynn; 62. The two women made the journey from Paterson, N.J.

They said they arrived on the island at 1 a.m., and came from the airport straight to the Capitol. Each woman was carrying a cardboard suitcase, one with a rope tied around it.

Sen, Ruth Fernández saw them there and, learning that they had made no plans for a place to stay, invited them to her home.

Mrs. Lynn said her daughter bought the women their roundtrip air tickets, "We have little money," said Mrs. Lynn, a native of Rio Grande, "so we bought the tickets on installment."

Mrs. Ayala, who was born in Yauco, said she went to join her step-sister, Mrs. Lynn, a year ago in New Jersey, where the latter has lived for the past 30 years.

"Why did we come back here?" Mrs. Ayala said. "Because Don Luis is dead. We are in debt to him for what he did for us. He always protected the poor," she said.

The two women said they would fly back to Patterson on Tuesday. Mrs. Fernández was making arrangements to have them taken to Barranquitas for Muñoz's funeral.

May 2, 1980

Crime, Corruption, Celebrities

*W*hile political status remained—and still remains—the island's seemingly never-ending conundrum, it never really made it to the top of the concerns of Puerto Rican voters in the 1960s-1980s. Islanders were more into the here-and-now of that time than in the possible political future. Crime usually led the polls as the island's top problem.

Most of the robberies and murders in those years were blamed on the illegal drug trade, which found fertile ground on the island, a major transshipment point for the South American cartels bringing drugs into the states. The criminals mostly, but not always, let tourists enjoy their sheltered visits. The bad guys did their thing mostly in the *caseríos*, the housing projects of the poor, and in the middle-class homes and stores around the island. If you were halfway vigilant, you knew what streets and areas to avoid at what times.

Several high-profile crimes captured the island's interest in those decades. Number one was Cerro Maravilla, where the cops were the criminals. Number two was the slaying of TV personality Luis Vigoreaux, who, a jury decided, was murdered in a contract killing taken out on him by his wife, actress Lydia Echevarría.

The Cerro Maravilla killings by police of two young *independentistas* occurred in 1978, on July 25—the day marked in Puerto Rico as the beginning of the Puerto Rico-U.S. "special" Commonwealth relationship, which began in 1952. The Cerro Maravilla case had reverberations down through the years.

At first, investigations by local and federal authorities, including the U.S. Justice Department's Civil Rights Division, produced no criminal charges in the slaying of the two young men, Arnaldo Darío Rosado, 24, and Carlos Soto Arriví, 18, *independentistas* who supposedly planned to blow up a communications tower on the Maravilla mountaintop. But, eventually, federal Grand Jury enquiries led to convictions of second-degree murder and perjury with prison terms of six to 30 years. Included in the group were the three officers who pulled the triggers after the victims surrendered, and were on their knees with their hands in the air.

The morning after the shootings, the officers had claimed they acted in self-defense, ordering Darío Rosado and Soto Arriví to surrender, and returning fire only after the two started the shooting. But police officers granted immunity subsequently told Puerto Rico Senate investigators that Darío Rosado and Soto Arriví had been beaten and killed after surrendering to as many as 20 officers who were lying in wait. The officers had learned that the two would be there from a police informer who had infiltrated the island independence group of the two young men.

The taxi driver who had taken Darío Rosado and Soto Arriví and the police informer to the site initially said he was under the dashboard of his cab when the shooting started and could not see who shot first. A few days later, in an interview with *San Juan Star* reporter Tomas Stella, the cabbie contradicted his statement, saying he ducked under the dashboard after the three men left the cab, and that he saw "10 heavily armed men" approaching. When he emerged from the car, he saw the three men alive and two of them were being beaten by the armed men, later identified as policemen.

Alejandro González Malavé, the undercover agent who was accompanying the *independentistas*, was not indicted for his part in the slayings; he was granted immunity for testifying against other officers, then removed from the police force. On the evening of April 29, 1986, González was assassinated in front of his mother's house in Bayamón. No one was ever charged with the killing. Romero's loss of his reelection bid in 1984 has been laid at least in part to his statement right after the incident that the police involved were "heroes." In 1992, former U.S. Justice Department Civil Rights Division Chief Drew S. Days III admitted before the Puerto Rico Senate that the federal Justice Department and the FBI acted negligently during the 1978-1980 investigations into the killings.

***

The Vigoreaux case came to trial in September, 1984, almost two years after the killing of the TV celebrity. The sensational trial was full of enough drama to attract coverage by stateside media. The mainland reports noted that Vigoreaux and Echevarría had been an extremely popular showbiz couple, and that the murder caused as much commotion on the island as if, say, Lucille Ball had taken out a contract on Desi Arnaz. Through its many twists and turns, the case became a real-life, murderous soap opera.

Vigoreaux and Echevarría had been married 20 years, and had co-hosted a popular weekly variety show. The tall, handsome Vigoreaux was reportedly very interested in a young actress and the 50-year-old Echevarría was reportedly angry enough to contact some local hitmen-druggies to put a permanent end to the affair.

Geraldo Rivera, of the then-popular TV news show "20-20," came to the island and interviewed me—I was covering the trial for the *Star*. Found guilty of arranging her husband's death, Echevarría was sentenced in 1986 to 209 years in prison. She was released in 1999 by then-Gov. Pedro Rosselló because of declining health. A curfew was placed on her activities--she had to be home by 8 p.m.—but she managed to partially resume her TV and stage careers.

Besides writing for the *Star*, I became a special correspondent for the *New York Daily News* in the late 1970s and the 1980s, filing stories about the island for, among others, the newspaper's growing New York Puerto Rican readership. Following are the stories about the Cerro Maravilla and the Vigoreaux cases that appeared in both the San Juan and New York newspapers.

8 Cops Charged in Slaying of 2

Utuado, P.R.—After more than six years, local authorities have brought murder charges against policemen involved in the July 25, 1978, shooting of two independence advocates who were killed on the Cerro Maravilla mountaintop near this central island town.

Utuado District Judge Ruth Miriam Pérez found probable cause Friday to charge eight policemen with two counts each of first-degree murder. Six of the eight also were accused of perjury in an alleged cover-up of the case, while murder and perjury charges against two other policemen were left pending.

Those accused of murder were freed on $20,000 bail.

The policemen already had been indicted by a federal grand jury for perjury and conspiracy to obstruct justice. Murder charges, however, could only be brought by the Commonwealth.

Gov. Carlos Romero Barceló said the delay in filing local charges was the fault of the Senate, controlled by the opposition Popular Democratic Party, which he said had withheld crucial evidence from the Commonwealth Justice Department.

Since 1981, the Senate has been investigating the slayings of Carlos Soto Arriví, 18, and Arnoldo Darío Rosado, 24. The two were slain in a police ambush while on an alleged terrorist mission to blow up communications towers.

While the official police version had maintained that the *independentistas* were killed only after they opened fire, the Senate hearings produced other evidence. Three policemen on the scene testified that an undercover agent led the two *independentistas* into a police trap, where they had been killed execution-style after they surrendered and fell to their knees to beg for mercy.

While previous investigations by the Commonwealth Justice Department and federal authorities had cleared the police of any wrongdoing, subsequent testimony before the Senate showed strong evidence of a cover-up by local law enforcement authorities.

Among those charged Friday were former Col.

Angel Pérez Casillas, then head of the police intelligence division that carried out the Cerro Maravilla operation. Also charged was former Capt. Jaime Quiles, who directed the operation.

The three policemen who testified at the Senate hearings about the murders had been given immunity from prosecution.

Popular Democratic Party gubernatorial candidate Rafael Hernández Colón called the filing of charges 17 days before the elections a "political show" and implied that the local Justice Department had built a weak case that could collapse in court. He said that if he were elected, he would strengthen the government's case by putting it in the hands of a special prosecutor.

The party, meanwhile, attempted to preclude any last-minute campaign mileage in the case for the Romero administration by placing full-page ads in the island's dailies. "If it hadn't been for the Senate of Puerto Rico," the ads read, "there would have no charges in the Cerro Maravilla case."

Oct. 21, 1984

Witness: Vigoreaux Alive Until Car Torched

In testimony rife with melodrama, Francisco "Papo" Newmann—the TV extra who took center stage Monday as the prosecution's star witness in the Luis Vigoreaux case—charged that actress Lydia Echevarría instigated her estranged husband's murder, which he carried out with co-defendant David López Watts.

Newmann, speaking at times in a barely audible voice, gave a startling account of Vigoreaux's slaying, his alleged affair with Echevarría and the cocaine habit that supposedly spurred him and López Watts into accepting money from the actress to "eliminate" the well-known TV personality.

He described to a packed, completely hushed courtroom in the San Juan Judicial Center in Hato Rey a macabre scene that seemed to come out of a horror movie. Newmann said that some minutes after Vigoreaux was stuffed in the trunk of his Mercedes Benz after being stabbed many times by López Watts with an ice pick, he went to the trunk to take out a suitcase that Echevarría had asked him to get.

Newmann testified that as he opened the car's trunk, Vigoreaux, who was thought dead, suddenly thrust out an arm and grabbed him tightly above the left wrist. The 36-year-old actor, who has appeared in TV commercials and soap operas, said he picked up a tire iron from the trunk and hit Vigoreaux twice over the head.

He took out the suitcase, Newmann said, and told López Watts, "We have to destroy everything." The two men got gasoline from a gas station and Newmann set the Mercedes on fire, he said.

Coroner Rafael Criado, who also testified Monday, reconfirmed his findings that Vigoreaux was still alive when the car was set on fire.

Newmann, who received immunity from prosecution in exchange for turning state's evidence, appeared before District Judge Gloria Iagrossi, who must decide after a preliminary hearing if enough evidence exists to try Echevarría and López Watts.

Both are charged with first-degree murder in the Vigoreaux slaying and with conspiring to murder actress Nydia Castillo, the entertainer's fiancée.

Dressed in a tailored gray suit and wearing stylish, thin-rimmed aviator glasses, Newmann said he first met Echevarría in late 1981 or early 1982 when the two appeared in the soap opera, "Viernes Social." He had a small part, he said.

He confirmed earlier testimony by other witnesses that some months before Vigoreaux's slaying, which occurred on the night of Jan. 17, 1983, he accompanied Echevarría to the Cupey Country Club for an artists' benefit. There, he said, he and Echevarría met Julio Andrades, the former police officer now serving a term in federal prison for hijacking and other crimes.

Newmann said Andrades, by then off the police force, presented them with his card and said he offered various services in his new business. Echevarría asked in a joking manner, Newmann said, if those services included "getting rid of someone."

"What did he (Andrades) answer?" asked Justice department attorney Luis Román.

"He laughed," said Newmann.

Newmann, however, alleged that he soon learned the actress was in earnest. He and Echevarría began an affair, he said, mentioning the places where they supposedly had sexual relations.

The actress first "asked me to eliminate Nydia Castillo," Newmann testified. He said he did not give her direct answer.

After an incident in which Vigoreaux supposedly offended" Vanessa Vigoreaux, his daughter by Echevarría, the actress asked Newmann to kill Vigoreaux also, according to the witness.

He said he told her he could not do it because "right now I have a cocaine habit and that is the only thing that occupies me." His habit, he said, was supported, among other ways, by selling stolen goods.

Newmann said he then recruited a long-time friend, López Watts, to carry out the slaying. The three supposedly finalized their plans to eliminate Vigoreaux and Castillo in a meeting at Echevarría's home in late December, 1982.

Newmann said Echevarría gave him a key to Vigoreaux's Mercedes Benz to get the suitcase she wanted from the trunk. They sealed the arrangement, he said, with drinks of scotch.

Newmann asserted that Echevarría soon after gave him $500. The payment was made, he said, at the home of the actress' mother, Julia Rodríguez. He said he split the money with López Watts for both to buy cocaine.

Newmann then gave the following version of what happened on the day Vigoreaux was murdered:

Echevarría called him in the morning to say she was meeting with Vigoreaux between 5 and 6 p.m. at her attorneys' office in El Centro Condominium in Hato Rey. The couple was in the process of getting a divorce.

Newmann then met with López Watts, who said he would accompany him to carry out the plan to kill Vigoreaux. But first, the two stopped at a public housing project for cocaine.

When Vigoreaux came out of the condominium, the two men followed him in López Watts' car to the Trujillo Alto road, believing he was on his way to fiancée Castillo's house.

While waiting for a traffic light on the road, Vigoreaux spotted Newmann and López Watts behind him. López Watts then told Newmann "forget Nydia." Newmann got out of López Watts's car and opened the door to the Mercedes with the key Echevarría had given him.

Newmann pulled out an ice pick he had taken from his mother's kitchen and told Vigoreaux, "Don't look around and do what I tell you."

Vigoreaux asked, "What's going on?"

Both cars then pulled over to a deserted spot and Newmann turned over the ice pick to López Watts, who repeatedly stabbed Vigoreaux.

In describing the incident of Vigoreaux reaching out from the trunk, Newmann said Vigoreaux's arm hung outside after he hit the TV entertainer on the head and closed the trunk again. He said he tried to pull the watch off Vigoreaux's wrist to sell for cocaine, but it would not come free. The incident, he said, greatly unnerved him.

In earlier testimony Monday, Marilyn Cintrón Brands, who said she was a former girlfriend of López Watts, testified that he came to her house on the night of the Vigoreaux slaying to ask for a container. López Watts said his friend needed to transfer gas to his car, Cintrón testified.

She said she gave him an empty plastic gallon bottle that once held "La Montaña" brand spring water. Such a bottle was earlier entered into evidence as being found at the site in Cupey where Vigoreaux's burned body and car were found.

Newmann testified that after getting the bottle, the two men filled it with gas from a gasoline station, then Newmann poured the gasoline over the car and set it afire.

Newmann's testimony that Vigoreaux was stabbed with an ice pick contradicts that of Criado, who said a barbecue fork was used as a weapon. The coroner based this, he said again Monday, on his findings that there were 10 pairs of stab wounds on Vigoreaux's body.

Coroner Criado said the perforations in each pair were parallel, in the same direction and uniformly separated by two centimeters. Justice attorney Román contested this, noting that on two of three samples of Vigoreaux's skin presented as evidence in court Monday, only one perforation could be seen.

Criado, who said photographs of the autopsy bear out his contention that a two-pronged instrument was used, acknowledged, however, that it was possible that an ice pick was used to kill Vigoreaux.

"In medicine," he said, "anything is possible."

July 23, 1985

**Lydia Echevarría and Luis Vigoreaux
holding local TV awards**

Dreams Of a Better Life

*I*t was called the "Showcase of Democracy" in the Sixties, but growing economic and social problems tarnished Puerto Rico's image somewhat in the following decades; yet for many residents of nearby Caribbean islands, emigrating to the U.S. Commonwealth was seen as the way to a better life.

***

The political crisis and civil war in the Dominican Republic included a U.S. invasion in 1965, four years after the assassination of Dominican dictator Rafael Trujillo, and two years following the overthrow by the military of Juan Bosch, the duly elected reformist president. Bosch, whose mother was Puerto Rican, went into exile in Puerto Rico in 1963. His overthrow led to political chaos as various groups, including the increasingly splintered military, struggled for power. By 1965, forces demanding the reinstatement of Bosch began attacks against the military-controlled government. The U.S. feared that "another Cuba" was in the making and President Lyndon Johnson sent more than 22,000 U.S. troops to "restore order" in the D.R. While other political figures and middle-class families followed Bosch into Puerto Rico exile, by far the largest number of the many thousand illegal Dominican immigrants who made it to Puerto Rico in the 1970s and 1980s were the poor, trying to escape the country's economic oppression.

Many of the illegal trips were made by *yola* (small wooden boat) across the Mona Passage that separated Puerto Rico from Hispaniola, the island shared by the Dominican Republic and Haiti. Several tragedies occurred during the dangerous 90-mile crossing, including a 1989 sinking near Mona Island where some 500 Dominican lives were reportedly lost.

A Dominican *yola*: overflowing with Cuban and Dominican refugees tries to cross the Mona Passage to enter Puerto Rico illegally. The boat was intercepted by the U.S. Coast Guard.

* * *

Haitian "immigration" to Puerto Rico became national news in August, 1981, when 125 illegal Haitian refugees were flown by the U.S. government from Miami to Juana Díaz. The refugees were brought to the former Fort Allen Navy Base from an overcrowded detention center in Miami, the first of subsequent flight that brought several hundred Haitians to the facility.

The New York Times reported then: "The Immigration and Naturalization Service, apparently expecting trouble on arrival here [at Fort Allen] . . . quietly put the refugees aboard a plane at 4 in the morning. There were no protesters, but several Puerto Ricans presented themselves at the gate of the new refugee center to apply for jobs."

The story continued: "Tonight a local group known as the United People's Committee called a demonstration outside Fort Allen, not to protest the Haitians' presence but what it termed the 'inhumane' way in which they were being treated. "The hot, treeless 10-acre plain on which they are to live, in tents surrounded by barbed wire, makes Puerto Ricans feel as though Washington is using Puerto Rico to do its dirty work," the committee said.

In December of that year, two members of Congress—one of whom was Rep. Robert (Bobby) García, D-N.Y., the second Puerto Rican ever elected to Congress (after Herman Badillo) made a "fact-finding" visit to Fort Allen. García strongly criticized the conditions at the former Army camp. I reported on their visit.

* * *

The largest immigration "influence" on the island undoubtedly was from the thousands of Cubans who made Puerto Rico their home in the decades following the Castro revolution. Some 20,000 Cuban exiles were living in Puerto Rico by the end of the 1980s, but nowhere near the 541,000 Cubans in Florida at that time, according to U.S, Census figures. Nevertheless, the many middle-class exile Cubans made considerable marks in Puerto Rico's business, entertainment and artistic fields. Many of the Cuban exiles' politics were more conservative than their more politically liberal hosts, yet much of their concerns for family, their humor and their deep-down humanity appeared to give credence to the words of Puerto Rican poet Lola Rodríguez de Tío that Cuba and Puerto Rico were "two wings of the same bird."

Some months after the column below that I wrote in 1986 about Patricia Gutiérrez, her father, Eloy Gutiérrez Menoyo, was released from prison after a petition from the Spanish government, which then had close ties with Cuba. Gutiérrez Menoyo went on to form *Cambio Cubano* in Miami, an organization that attempted a dialogue between the Castro government and its exile opponents. He was actually allowed to move back to Cuba in 2003, where he tried to get Castro to allow *Cambio Cubano* to function as an opposition party. That never happened. Gutiérrez-Menoyo died in Havana in 2012 at age 77. Patricia Gutiérrez become the director of a publishing company in Puerto Rico.

'Stalag 17' Sapping Spirit of Haitian Refugees

Most of the bad things you have been hearing and reading about Fort Allen are true. I was there. And I came away feeling sad and upset and angry over the conditions in which the Haitians are living.

The 743 refugees now there—583 males, including an 11-year-old and two teenagers, and 160 females—are given the bare necessities, almost nothing else. They are adequately fed and clothed and they have access to a modern medical clinic at the former Navy communications station.

The recently reported cases of breast enlargement among males may, in fact be due to an improvement in the way the refugees are eating. Similar symptoms have been detected in underfed males who suddenly receive a balanced diet, according to Dr. Yamil Kouri of the Commonwealth Health Department.

So the Haitians at Fort Allen are not suffering physically. Their suffering is confined to the spirit, to those conditions that shrivel the soul of humans everywhere.

They are penned up behind barbed wire and given little to do to relieve their mounting despair. They realize the U.S. government wants to send them back to Haiti. It has to be a measure of the miserableness of their lives in Haiti that the vast majority has withstood pressure to "volunteer" to go back. (Refugees have told reporters of daily announcements over the camp public address system urging them to return to Haiti.)

I was at Fort Allen to cover the fact-finding visit of Rep. Robert García, D-N.Y., and Rep. Mary Rose Oakar, D-Ohio. Contrary to past policy of the Immigration and Naturalization Service, this time reporters had few restrictions placed on them.

We sat in on a briefing of the Congress members and their staffs, then visited the medical clinic. Then we began a tour of the refugees' compound, driving up in a bus to the guarded gate. (There are some 380 armed guards at the camp, the legislators were told, which led García to say almost unbelievingly. "That's about one guard for every two Haitians!")

The gate was opened and we drove down a dirt road between chain link fences. Atop these fences were coils of barbed wire with large, vicious-looking fish hooks enmeshed in the wire. The hooks seemed capable of ripping the body of anyone trying to climb over.

Behind the barbed wire, under the watchful eye of the armed guards, stood the Haitians, the same people described by an INS official at the briefing as "docile." They stared at the passing bus with a mixture of apathy and hope. Some waved tentatively, others shrugged and turned up their palms in a wordless plea that cut across any language barrier. These were the people who came searching for freedom in the United States and wound up in this treeless, overheated, baked earth (now rain-muddy) compound that looked for all the world like Stalag 17.

We ate lunch with the refugees—codfish, rice, salad, bread, margarine, canned peaches and coffee. The Haitians—at first diffidently, then more boldly, began talking to us, either in halting English, or Spanish, or

in French or Creole through an interpreter. They poured out their stories. Most said if they went back to Haiti they would be in very big trouble. They claimed to be political exiles.

Evidently, they have learned a lot during their four months at Fort Allen. They learned that their only hope of remaining in the United States is to claim political asylum.

When 17 Haitians were rescued from sea last July and brought to Puerto Rico, they were told they could ask for political asylum. The term confused them. They insisted they weren't communists, if that's what political asylum meant.

Now the Haitians know enough to tell visiting congressmen and reporters that they are, indeed, political exiles.

During the lunch, Jean-Louis (not his real name) came forward to boldly proclaim to García in English that the refugees were living in terrible conditions. He invited the congressman to inspect the tents where the refugees live. Jean-Louis was confident and articulate and he looked sharp in a white jump suit and stood up man-to-man to García's tough questioning.

García, who was called to mediate, among other prison

riots, the Attica affair, said later that he has seen the same thing over and over, natural leaders like Jean-Louis springing up among people in adverse circumstances.

We visited the barrack-like tents. There were beds and sheets, but the refugees were provided with absolutely nothing for their meager belongings, There were no clothes racks, no footlockers, no hangers, no pegs, no hooks.

Nothing to hang a shirt, or a hope, on.

Clothes were strung along rope and some of the men had cardboard boxes by their bedside. The women fared somewhat better. They had makeshift bedside stands covered with colorful paper, jars and bottles on top of the stands.

The legislators were upset when the refugees told them that families had been separated in the transfer from Krome North in Miami to Fort Allen. They also learned that common-law spouses were separated at the Juana Diaz camp.

García went away calling Fort Allen "a prison" and saying that Haitians were being treated worse than any immigrants to the United States ever have been because they are black. Rep, Oakar found the fort "concentration camp-like," where the Haitians were being kept "like caged animals."

Fort Allen really is a miserable place that exudes despair. There are more humane ways to enforce immigration laws than treating human beings with disdain so they will want to go back home and others will be discouraged from trying to come into the country.

The INS should be made to reunite families. It should set up quarters for common-law spouses to live together. It should improve conditions at the camp immensely or release the Haitians in the custody of local families who have volunteered to take them in.

Most important, the Reagan administration should recognize that the Haitian refugees are victims of a corrupt and tyrannical political system that has kept them in crushing poverty, and that if they return home, the political-economic persecution will continue. The government should realize that the Haitians meet the qualifications for political asylum.

Dec. 20, 1987

Father-Daughter Bond Transcends Cuban Prison

"Although I know you must be a woman by now, to me you will always be my little girl. That is the image that remains fresh in my mind and the one that has occupied me every second, like a day of sunshine, in the darkest moments."

The above is from a letter by a father to his daughter, who he has learned will soon marry. The father gives his permission and blessings for the marriage. The letter was received by the daughter on Aug. 5, the first word she has had from her father in several years.

The daughter, Patricia Gutiérrez, 24, lives in Puerto Rico, She works for a local publishing firm, and will wed in February. The father Eloy Gutiérrez Menoyo 52, resides in the Boniato Prison in Cuba's Oriente Province. He has spent the last 21 years, 7 months in Fidel Castro's prisons, since he was captured in January, 1965 after trying to infiltrate Cuba and overthrow the Castro regime.

Gutiérrez has not seen his daughter since she was six months old. She has no memory of his physical being, yet he is in her thoughts, she says, every day of her life. She is her father's only child.

"Each day I do something to try to get him out of prison," she said in an interview the other day. "At the least, I spend an hour writing one more letter or I call one more person. I don't feel any government has a right to keep your parent away from you, especially for so long."

"It's awful because I know I have a father. I know where he is and I can't get to him. I don't feel free because I cannot get to see the person I most want to see in life," she said.

Castro's Victims is the title of an article in the July 17 New York Review of Books, a liberal weekly publication. It was written by Aryeh Neier, Vice Chairman of the Helsinki Watch Committee and American Watch Committee, both human rights monitoring organizations.

Neier writes: "Since Fidel Castro took power in 1959, Cuba has confined large numbers of political prisoners for longer periods than any other country in the world...many of the political prisoners were confined in a long period under the degrading and cruel circumstances.

Eloy Gutiérrez is one of Castro's victims. His daughter has learned from former prisoners that he has been in solitary confinement for the past 15 years, an electric bulb his only source of light in that time; that since 1971 he has been refused visiting, writing and letter-receiving privileges; that he has become deaf in one ear and blind in one eye and has developed bleeding ulcers; that he has been kept naked since 1971, the year he refused to put on the uniform of a common criminal, as decreed by Castro. Gutiérrez is a *plantado,* a prisoner who refuses to be rehabilitated, Castro-style.

Gutiérrez has fought against Cuban dictator Fulgencio Batista in a group similar to Castro's July 26th movement. His family, in fact, has a history of fighting against dictators. His father, Carlos Gutiérrez Zabaleta, was a cofounder of the Spanish Socialist Party. The elder Gutiérrez fought in the Spanish Civil War, as did Eloy Gutiérrez' oldest brother, José Antonio, who was killed trying to defend the Republic against the Franco forces.

The family survivors, including the teenage Eloy, left Spain after several unbearable years under Franco. During World War II, Carlos, another brother, joined the Free French and marched with General Leclerc into a liberated Paris.

The family settled in Cuba in 1948. In 1957, brother Carlos joined a rebel group that stormed the presidential palace. He was cut down by the Batista forces, the second son to give up his life in a fight against dictatorship.

Eloy Gutiérrez, who owned a small night spot in Havana, became "radicalized" against Batista after his brother's death and joined in the struggle against the dictator. Soon after Castro took power, Gutiérrez sensed one more dictatorship on the horizon and he left Cuba. Six months after Patricia was born, he left his wife and child behind in Miami to go to training bases, according to his diary, in Puerto Rico and the Dominican Republic.

He then made the unsuccessful attempt to ignite an anti-Castro revolution and was sentenced to 65 years in prison.

The letter came to Patricia on August 5 in the same convoluted way that Gutiérrez learned of his daughter's imminent marriage. The means of the "exchange" will not be described here to protect the innocent.

Patricia's next to last communication with her father, in 1978, occurred when a thin volume appeared mysteriously in her mailbox while she was living in Miami. Written in purple ink on both sides of 20 pages of onion skin paper, in minute, filigreed script, was a children's story. The story is about a bird who saves the hero from drowning. The story was clandestinely composed by Gutiérrez for Patricia as a fifteenth birthday present. She has since had it published.

Patricia said she had received letters from her father fairly regularly until 1971, when she was nine years old. "I didn't understand why I wasn't getting letters anymore," she said. She opened a red jewelry box filled with her father's letters and other papers related to his life. "This is my dad to me," she said. The letters were filled with drawings of little angels and palm beaches and Cuban flags. "He would always put something pretty in them," Patricia said.

She said that since about age 15, when she was mature enough, she has appealed for her father's freedom. Her mother remarried seven years ago in an attempt at a new life. Patricia continues writing letters to popes, presidents and others.

Since Gutiérrez was born and raised in Spain, and because of his family's widely known anti-Franco activities, his continued imprisonment has become a *cause célèbre* in that country. Patricia has gone to Spain to work for her father's release. Sen. Edward Kennedy, D-Mass., also has lent support. In April, he wrote a letter to Fidel Castro on behalf of Gutiérrez.

"Surely the interest of justice has been served by 22 years in incarceration," wrote the senator. Castro has not answered the letter. Kennedy wrote Patricia, however, to say that, "I have been told that Castro will give full consideration to my request."

Kennedy got involved after Patricia crashed a reception for him at the Condado Beach Hotel earlier this year. She had been corresponding with the senator's office for the past two years, but now she wanted to deliver a letter personally to Kennedy. She sat for two hours waiting to talk to the Senator until a Kennedy aide told her to get on the end of a long reception line.

"I guess she (the aide) felt sorry for me," Patricia said.

The aide introduced her to Kennedy. "My hand was in his and I wouldn't let go."

'Believe me,' Kennedy said, 'The United States is doing everything within its reach to get your dad out."

I didn't believe that and started crying. His eyes got watery and he cut out the bull and told me, 'I'll try to do my best.' I could tell by the way he said it that he finally committed himself."

Patricia Gutiérrez said: "I'm not selfish. I want to hug my dad just once."

Aug. 17, 1986

Eloy Gutiérrez Menoyo shares a moment with his three-month-old daughter, Patricia, in 1962.

Editor's Note: Patricia managed an exchange of hugs with her father on Dec. 22, 1986 in a Madrid airport lounge after Eloy Gulierrez Menoyo was released from prison in Cuba and put on a flight to Spain.

Wars: Current
and Future

*T*he Vietnam War, of course, had repercussions on the
island. Some 48,000 Puerto Ricans from the island and
the states served in that U.S. war. Reported Puerto Rican
casualties: 455 killed and 3,775 wounded. There were protests on the island against the war; in 1973, two members of
the Puerto Rican Legislature —Sen. Rubén Berríos and Rep.
Carlos Gallisá, both supporters of island independence—introduced legislation condemning the war and calling for a
U.S. withdrawal from Vietnam. The legislation was defeated
as the Puerto Rico government appeared to go out of its way
to avoid any conflict with Washington over the war.

There were many island demonstrations against the war
and even official signs of compassion to the war's opponents. In 1970, Federal Court Judge Hiram Cancio, appoint-
ed by President Johnson who was irretrievably tied to the
war—made a headline-getting decision when he symbolically sentenced a conscientious objector to imprisonment for
one hour. The judge, a World War II veteran, suggested the
defendant serve his sentence in the U.S. Marshal's Office in
the courthouse building in Old San Iran.

Then there was Sergeant First Class Jorge Otero Barreto of Vega Baja, who happened to serve five tours in Southeast Asia and became the U.S. military's most decorated soldier of the war. Starting as an advisor who helped train Vietnamese troops, Otero Barreto earned 38 decorations, including three Silver Stars, five Bronze Stars, five Purple Hearts four Army Commendation Medals, and five Air Medals. He served in the U.S. Army from 1961 to 1970 and participated in 200 combat missions.

The war officially ended April 30, 1975.

* * *

At different times in the 20th century, the U.S. had about 25 military or naval installations in Puerto Rico. These included the former Roosevelt Roads Naval Station in Ceiba, which was the Navy's largest base in the world, and, of course, the Atlantic Fleet Weapons Training Facility (AFWTF) on Vieques. While the battle to get the Navy to withdraw from Vieques lasted into the 21st Century (the Navy stopped its maneuvers there in 2003), the Vieques protests actually started getting U.S. federal court notice in the late 1970s, after the Navy quit using the smaller offshore island of Culebra (in 1975) for its bombing and strafing maneuvers.

Back in the 1940s, the Navy took over two-thirds of Vieques—22,000 acres of the 33,000-acre-island. About 8,000 acres on the western end of the island was primarily used as a naval ammunition depot, while 14,000 acres on the eastern end was used for live training exercises. These exercises included ship-to-shore gunfire, air-to-ground bombing and amphibious landings. Within that area was a 900-acre

Live Impact Area used for targeting live ordnance. The locals lived between the depot and the live ammo shelling and bombing and the sounds, and sometimes damages, of "war" were a daily occurrence.

Demonstrations to get the Navy to stop the live-fire maneuvers went on through the 1970s and 1980s. The issue took off when in April 1999, a Navy bomber misfired its missiles at a practice range and struck the main watch-post on the island, killing David Sanes Rodríguez, a Vieques resident and civilian employee of the Navy. The protests that followed gathered international attention.

The Navy left Vieques on May 1, 2003.

Protesters against the Navy's live-fire maneuvers
on Vieques march July 4, 1999 outside the gates of
the Roosevelt Roads Naval Base in Ceiba.

The Legislature and Vietnam

At long last, voices within the "establishment" have spoken out in Puerto Rico against what all the world—except certain segments of official Washington, official Saigon and official San Juan—admits is the U.S.'s most monstrous hour: the insane war it is waging in Vietnam.

Almost one decade and millions of lives later (several hundred of which have been Puerto Rican), the Legislature of Puerto Rico has before it a resolution actually critical of U.S. action in what has to be one of the most harshly treated lands and people in the five million or so years men have had the opportunity to bludgeon one another into submissiveness.

The resolution, which calls for U.S. withdrawal from Vietnam, was introduced by the new legislators of the Puerto Rican Independence Party. Of course, it would have to be the *independentistas* who bring up the issue. Politicians of the other ideologies have been lacking in interest, concern or guts to make public statements on America's greatest disgrace. The statehood-orientated blindly accept and praise just about anything the U.S. does in foreign relations, while the Commonwealthers, especially when in power, are unwilling to ruffle the eagle's feathers, the one that lays the golden federal-aid egg up in Washington.

The only collective utterance by establishment politicians on the matter occurred on Feb. 3, 1966. On that day, the Legislature all but unanimously approved a resolution giving President Johnson Puerto Rico's undying support (undying in the case of the island's legislators, if not its conscriptees) of his prosecution of the war. Only the Popular Democratic Party's Sen. José Arsenio Torres voted against the resolution.

So now the PIP legislators have to remind us of that day. As Sen. Rubén Berríos pointed out Monday while announcing the PIP-sponsored anti-Vietnam proposal at a press conference: "The Puerto Rican Legislature is the only legislature in the world to have endorsed the criminal war in Vietnam."

And as when the paranoid said, "Just because I think I'm being followed doesn't mean

I'm not," so too, just because the PIP legislators say the U.S. action in Vietnam is criminal doesn't mean it isn't.

The horror of a war in which babies burn to save one president's or another's face is too much to accept, too much to read about any more or talk about, even to write about. No one will ever be able to rationally explain a Lt. Calley; no one should be able to. Monstrous crimes have a demonic logic all their own.

The Puerto Rico Legislature now has an. opportunity to redeem itself and show that the politicians of Puerto Rico, who supposedly speak; for the Puerto Rican people, can and will speak up for life and against what has become U.S.-sanctioned genocide. The legislators should ask themselves this: what if those thousands of maimed babies were Puerto Rican?

Nov. 4, 1981

UPR: Politics and Culture

*T*he University of Puerto Rico played a pivotal role in the politics of the island in the l960s-1980s with multiple student demonstrations, bureaucratic clashes and one unforgettable tragedy.

Most people on the island at the time will always remember the name of Antonia Martínez Lagares, the 21-year-old student who was shot and killed by police while she stood on the second-floor balcony of her student residence in Rio Piedras watching a demonstration going on below. It was March 4, 1970, a time when campus protests against the Vietnam War were taking place throughout the U.S. The UPR demonstration on that day was against the Reserve Officers Training Corps (ROTC) program. The ROTC prepared students to enter the armed services as officers. Antonia Martínez Lagares watched as police began beating fellow students and she shouted at them *"asesinos!"* (assassins). One of the policemen reportedly looked up to the balcony, then shot her. The young woman became a martyr in the anti-Vietnam War movement in Puerto Rico.

Still, there were times when the methods used by the students in their other protests, while mostly done for the right reasons, took wrong turns for some of their peers. Below is one account, of a tuition strike in 1981 that seemed to go awry.

The UPR was also a cultural center for the island. The great Spanish Cellist Pablo Casals, who made the island his home after taking refuge from the Franco dictatorship, organized conducted and played in the yearly Casals Festival at the UPR Theater. The festival featured classical music greats from around the world. Below is a 90th birthday interview I did of Casals for *The New York Times*.

There was also a film club that showed some of the most important movies of the era that were not shown in commercial theaters—from *The Battle of Algiers* about France's unsuccessful efforts to hold onto its Algerian colony, to *Memories of Underdevelopment*, a nuanced Cuban film about the revolution. Local and visiting artists and writers held classes and gave talks.

Among the visitors was Peruvian writer Mario Vargas Llosa, who gave classes at Río Piedras in 1986. Vargas Llosa won the Nobel Prize for Literature in 2010, becoming the third visiting author-professor at UPR to have won the highest literary honor. The other two were Spanish author Juan Ramón Jiménez, who was a professor for several years at the UPR starting in 1950 and won the award in 1956, and American writer Saul Bellow, who taught at the Rio Piedras campus in 1961 and won the Nobel Prize in 1976.

Mob Invades UPR Classroom

(Reporter Robert Friedman was sitting in Mrs. Margaret Inserni's English class Tuesday morning. This is his account of what happened.)

At 11:10 a.m. Tuesday the seven students who showed up for Margaret Inserni's expository writing class at the University of Puerto Rico were taking a practice exam on punctuation when the mob arrived.

First, a mild-mannered young man came up to the front of the room and made a speech. Then two or three of his compatriots walked to the Miami windows and shut the louvers. Then another young man erased the classroom lesson on the blackboard and wrote across it: HUELGA (strike). Then someone shut off the lights, leaving the room on the first floor of the Humanities Building at Rio Piedras in semi-darkness.

Then the mob moved in—first 10, then 20, then 30 and perhaps 40 of them—clapping in unison, shouting, "Huelga! Huelga!" whistling, stamping their feet.

Of the seven students—six of whom were young women—three got up and left. Four female students remained with their teacher, Mrs. Inserni, a white-haired English professor who has taught on and off at UPR for 23 years.

Despite the darkness and the shouting, the students kept their heads bent to the papers in front of them, reading or pretending to read, occasionally making notes. Mrs. Inserni sat to the side of her desk, looking away.

One of the mob sat on the teacher's desk. Others sat in empty classroom seats. Still others formed a semicircle around the students, clapping, chanting, whistling.

The four young female students, looking small and vulnerable, remained in their seats, saying nothing. Their teacher didn't budge either.

The mob raised the noise level. Several males moved closer to the young women, standing over them, clapping in unison, whistling. They kept it up for about 15 minutes.

The four young women stuck it out. They refused to be intimidated.

Someone set off a stinkbomb nearby. Then the mob departed.

To an observer, it was not so much a frightening experience as it was a degrading one, to see a white-haired teacher and four young women subjected to the boisterousness, if not violence, of the mob of 40.

The attempt to break up the class was one of many that have taken place at the UPR Rio Piedras Campus since students began striking there two months ago over a tuition hike. These attempts have picked up again in the past few days, since police were removed from the campus.

The strikers nailed shut the doors of some classrooms in the Humanities Building Monday when students and teachers refused to leave. The administration removed the doors to the classrooms Tuesday so the act could not be repeated. Students in some classes barricaded the doorless entrances to their rooms, after entering them, with chairs piled on desks.

The strikers managed to disrupt, among others, several 7 a.m. English classes in the basement of the Humanities Building. They shut off the electricity, leaving the basement in darkness, jammed classroom door locks and threw stinkbombs, according to several English professors whose classes were disrupted.

Mrs. Inserni said she did not leave the classroom nor dismiss her students when the mob entered because, "I thought, 'this is my space and I'm not moving.' I don't think I can go along with this rabble-rousing."

She added: "Two professors came up to me after and said, 'Why did you resist? I told them, 'I'm not resisting, I'm staying where I belong.' "

Cristina Guerra, one of the students who refused to leave Mrs. Inserni's class, said she stayed on "to urge the 19,000 students who don't favor the strike to do what we did."

Miss Guerra, a petite 21-year-old education major, said while her parents can afford the tuition increase, if the university closed down, they would not be able to afford the tuition for her at a private university.

"The only place I can study is here," she said, then added: "Besides, it's the best university on the island, the only one that has strict entrance requirements.

"I'm proud of studying at the UPR," she said.

Nov. 4, 1981

Casals at 90: 'Life is Wonderful. Memories Can Enrich'

San Juan – Pablo Casals, almost 90, widened his pale blue eyes, pushed a forefinger into the air and said, "Fantastic!" Think what we have lost because Bach and Beethoven and Mozart and Schubert did not live to an old age. Bach was 65 when he died. I am 25 years older than that. Beethoven died at 57. Mozart was in his thirties. And Schubert was only 31.

"No one thinks about that. What they could have written!" He shook his finger at me emphatically. "Fantastic!"

Which could be the very word to utter when one observes the persisting vigor displayed by the Spanish-born musician, who will celebrate his 90th birthday on Thursday. For he shows few signs of slowing down and expresses even less desire to do so. Although the highlight of his birthday celebration will be a tribute at the Governor's mansion in San Juan, the world began honoring Casals on his 90th birthday last summer in France, where many of his countrymen came from Spain bearing gifts and musical offerings; and in Puerto Rico, almost every week, there is new homage to the musician.

"Because at my age, I cannot say I am absolutely well," Casals said during an interview at his beachfront home in the Isla Verde section of San Juan. "But I am well enough to continue my duties as a musician and as a human being."

The cellist said he feels no different from the way he did two, three or five years ago. "I continue to work the whole day. I continue to smoke my pipe. [Bits of tobacco on his short-sleeved white sport shirt attested to that.] I am still interested in everything."

His attractive 30-year-old Puerto Rican wife Marta added, "Thank God he hasn't diminished one bit in his activities. It's amazing." Mrs. Casals, who married The Maestro – as she constantly calls him – nine years ago, sat at the side of her husband, who leaned back on a green satin-covered couch, puffing, refilling, relighting his pipe.

Casals' daily activities still include an early morning walk along the beach, a piano homage to Bach (he plays each day from the preludes and fugues), cello practice, composing and teaching. This year, as always, he plans to participate fully in the San Juan and Prades music festivals in his honor, to teach classes at Marlboro, Vt., and to conduct in several countries his peace oratorio, *El Pesebre* (The Manger).

He spoke of upcoming travel with the enthusiasm of a college student planning his first year abroad. "There will be no slow-down in traveling in the coming year. There are many, many places where they want me to give the oratorio – Russia, Poland, Canada, Brazil, Korea, cities in the United States and Europe." No dates have been set yet. "For one thing, I can't stand the cold weather, so my traveling is reduced to the warm months. But I don't think of retiring. When a man reaches a certain age, he can begin to die by thinking too much of the fact that he is getting old. An old man should think of what has gone before in his life. Life is a wonderful thing. Memories can enrich."

Casals also has plans for bringing classical concerts to the working people of Puerto Rico. He said the arrangement would be much the same as in Barcelona during the twenties, when he helped establish the Workingmen's Concert Association. The Association members paid annual dues of about 50 cents and were entitled to attend 12 special Sunday morning concerts. Soloists of international repute, including Casals himself, performed.

"I am not satisfied with giving music only to people who have money to attend regular concerts. I want also to give it to people of limited resources – workers, students and the like. I am now talking with union leaders here of the necessity form giving the best music to the working people in Puerto Rico. They have a right to it and they need it."

Casals said the labor officials to whom he has already spoken were enthusiastic. "I would like to start again in Puerto Rico what, because of the civil war, was stopped by Spain," the native of Catalonia declared. "This sort of thing should, in fact, be done throughout the world." Once more he lit his pipe, as though symbolically rekindling life's flame for the full year ahead.

Giving the Puerto Rican workers the "best music" will mean – as it always means for Casals – giving them a generous helping of Bach. Casals remembers happily that Bach was the favorite among the Spanish laborers. "They understood good music by instinct. Music is like the word. I must understand every word you say to comprehend your meaning. Music must be the same. The fundamental laws of music don't change, just as natural feelings don't' change. The most important of these laws is to be sincere. The same as in life. But now in music, they want to be original. Most don't want to say they feel and they are afraid of being sincere."

"They" undoubtedly are the modern composers, a category which, for Casals, takes in most of his contemporaries and all who have arrived after with such sounds as those produced by serial, electronic and aleatoric music. But The Maestro did have fine words for many contemporary musicians. "The musicians of today – I mean the good ones – play better than the musicians of 50 years ago. They have mastered technique and have corrected, in many ways, the bad habits that had lasted until my youth. For example, at that time the wind instrumentalists and even the most celebrated artists of the string instruments

did not really play in tune. They say that Eugene Ysaye was the first violinist and I was the first cellist to play in tune – that is, as much as I was able to. I've always wondered how the orchestras must have sounded in the times of Bach and Beethoven."

As is inevitable in an interview with any of the great patriarchs of the age – Schweitzer, Einstein, Bertrand Russell or Casals – questions were asked about hope for the future of mankind. "I am an optimist, because what exists now is unnatural. By and by governments will see the necessity of getting together. I don't see how the world can survive if it repeats the cruelties of the recent past. The concept of war is unjustifiable. Values must change. They must be elevated to a point where war is considered unthinkable."

I sat with pencil poised, reluctant to make notes of the last statements, waiting for some brand new insight on correcting mankind's tragic flaw of seeking peace through war. "War must be considered unthinkable," Casals repeated. "Put that down!" he added passionately.

December 25, 1966

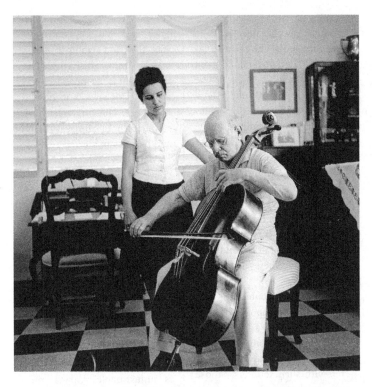

Pablo Casals plays his cello at his home in the Isla Verde
section of San Juan while his wife, Marta looks on.

An Afternoon with Mario Vargas Llosa

Antonio Luis Ferré, publisher of *El Nuevo Día*, was wandering around having a hard time finding a seat. So were lots of other people. High-class looking women in designer dresses and pearl necklaces sat on the carpeted floor, while others leaned against the walls. The amphitheater at the University of Puerto Rico's Education Department building was packed with professors, Miramar-type matrons, college students with piles of books, girls in high school uniforms, literary-leaning lawyers and assorted others. Females predominated by about 10 to 1.

Two TV cameras were set up at opposite ends of the amphitheater. Tape recorders were ready to roll. The room was buzzing with excitement. Why all the hubbub? Who was the object of all this ready-to-be-released admiration? Was it a salsa superstar, a TV actor, an *honest* politician? No, the enthusiastic turnout was for a fellow who puts words on paper, Mario Vargas Llosa, the Peruvian novelist, one of Latin America's—the world's—leading literary lights.

His latest book, "The Real Life of Alejandro Mayta," was reviewed on the front page of *The New York Times* book review section two Sundays ago; last Sunday, a feature by him about his son's Rastafarian period was the page one story in *The Times'* magazine; a play of his opened (to mixed reviews) two weeks ago on West 42nd Street in New York.

Meanwhile, Vargas Llosa, who turns 50 in March, is spending February at the UPR. He is being paid $20,000 for his four-week appearance, a sum criticized as excessive in some quarters in these hard funding times. But he is packing 40 hours of classes, conferences and conversations around the island into his visit. This includes seven sessions open to the public, Mondays and Wednesdays, 1 p.m. to 4 p.m., during which he talks about his life, his times, his works, the creative process. He spends the breaks autographing copies of his books brought up to him by admirers. And judging from one of the session's last week, the man is putting in quality time.

You remember seeing other writers, mostly from the U.S., stammering through self-appraisals of their works in one-hour lectures, and you wonder at the wonder of a writer lecturing 21 hours on his own literary output. But you have not taken into account that the great Latin American writers apparently are as eloquently loquacious as their prose is abundantly rich.

Vargas Llosa's steps into the amphitheater, wearing a short-sleeved guayabera. He puts on half glasses, pours himself a glass of water, offers a toothy smile, a lock of hair curling down one side of his forehead, and is often running.

"In the last class, we talked about '*Pantaleón y las visitadoras*,' and now I'm going to talk about *Aunt Julia and the Scriptwriter*. This book apparently is more autobiographical than my others. But not really."

For three hours, minus a fifteen-minute break, the writer becomes a non-stop talker. He stays seated behind a table on a small stage, but there is action in his expressive voice. He speaks enthusiastically, entertainingly, throws in some anecdotes. He speaks of art and

reality and truth and fiction and how they interrelate with the writer and his words. Take, for instance, "Aunt Julia."

The novel is a comic gem about a young man, who happens to be named Mario Vargas Llosa starting out as a news broadcaster. At the radio station, he meets a dwarf-life Bolivian, a man who dedicates his every waking (and probably sleeping) hour to the intense, serious, disciplined, maniacal pursuit of his art: the writing of soap operas. At the same time, eighteen-year-old Mario falls in love, and marries, his Aunt Julia, fourteen years his senior – just as the real-life Vargas Llosa's first marriage was with an older woman, causing soap-opera scandal in his family. In real life. And in a novel.

Some critics who can't see very far, see "Aunt Julia" as a lightweight performance, compared to Vargas Llosa's other works, which have taken on the weightier themes of religion, revolution, violence, political fanaticism – not to mention attempts by the author at the "total novel." The final word, or words, about the nitty and gritty of life created between the covers of a book.

Vargas Llosa said that when he started writing "Aunt Julia," he wanted to introduce his re-al-life story into that of Pedro Camacho, the Bolivian script-writer, whose aggressively wilder soap opera fantasies are related in every other chapter. "I wanted to make that part (his, Vargas Llosa's, story) true to my memories. But from the begin-ning, it wasn't possible to do it," the writer said. "You really can't just put real life into words. The narrator has to insert little lies to make the written truth more real. To be faithful to the grand design, "many modifications" had to be made in the details.

"Literature has its own real-ity," said Vargas Llosa. "Truth in literature is one thing, truth in life is something else."

He spoke about his "fascina-tion" for the world of the soap opera. Yes, it is "subliterature," but there is a type of reality in all the unreal goings-on that is truly Latin American.

Part Two of the class dealt with the background for *The War at the End of the World*, the novel of an uprising in 19th century Brazil. As Vargas Llosa relates the apoc-alyptic visions, the obsessions, the ideological distortions, the incredible adventures, the radical extremisms, the monstrosities, the dogmas, the phantasms, the soul-searching search for truth within that historic event-turned fictional reality, you wonder at the wonder of Latin American history. And of the writers who have turned it into the magical truth of their fiction.

Feb. 24, 1986

Mario Vargas Llosa in 1985

Island Tragedies

*F*our major tragedies—two of them occurring on separate New Year's Eves—took place on the island in the years being covered here. Two involved the death of single individuals while the others took many lives.

On Dec. 31, 1972, all-time baseball great Roberto Clemente was aboard a cargo plane on a mercy mission to Nicaragua, which had been hit by an earthquake weeks before. Just after takeoff, the plane crashed into the ocean off Isla Verde.

Clemente, who had visited Nicaragua just weeks before the quake hit, was on the plane because he learned that aid packages he had arranged to be put on three previous flights never reached the victims, but were diverted by officials in the corrupt Nicaraguan government of Anastasio Somoza. He hoped that his presence on the fourth relief flight would mean the cargo would be delivered to the victims.

Many Puerto Ricans spent that New Year's Eve on the Isla Verde beach, hoping that Clemente would somehow resurface. His body was never found.

Clemente, born in the island town of Carolina, was an All-Star for twelve seasons, the National League's most valuable player in 1961, 1964, 1965, and 1967, and the best fielder in his outfield position for 12 consecutive seasons. He batted over .300 for thirteen seasons and had 3,000 major league hits. And perhaps his lasting legacy: he was always involved in charity work in Latin American and Caribbean countries during the off-seasons, often delivering baseball equipment and food to those in need.

Clemente's widow, Vera said in interviews after her 38-year-old husband's death that he had told her several times that he thought he was going to die young. When Clemente was congratulated after his 3,000th hit and asked about his future, he told the interviewer: "Well, you never know... If I'm alive, like I said before, you never know because God tells you how long you're going to be here. So you never know what can happen tomorrow."

Below is an interview I did many years later in Washington, D.C. with Pulitzer Prize-winning writer David Maraniss about his 2006 biography of Clemente, which showed the baseball star's burgeoning greatness as a deeply human being.

**

On March 22, 1978, at age 73, Karl Wallenda, patriarch of the Flying Wallendas, the world-famous family of high-wire performers, plunged to his death in San Juan. He was attempting a walk across a wire stretched 120-feet above the pavement between the two towers of the ten-story Condado Plaza Hotel on Ashford Avenue in the tourist Condado section. As he was crossing, a gust of high wind blowing off the nearby ocean suddenly caused him to totter on the wire then fall to his death on the pavement below as a crowd of tourists, and others, looked on in horror. My story below, a rewrite of several reports since I wasn't on the scene of the accident, ran in the *New York Daily News.*

* * *

In the middle of the night of Oct. 7, 1985, as most residents slept in their shanty homes in Barrio Mameyes outside Ponce, the island's second largest city, a massive mudslide tumbled over the homes, taking hundreds of lives (reports had put the death toll at 130 to as many as 300). It was, at the time, the deadliest landslide in U.S. history.

In addition to the deadly landslide in Mameyes, floods washed out a bridge in Santa Isabela that killed several people. The storm system caused about $125 million in damages.

In a very strange addendum, three days before the Mameyes landslide, a group of children from a nearby Head Start school reportedly were asked by their teacher to draw "whatever came to their minds." Several of them made drawings that featured crosses, and dark earth-like colors, which have been interpreted by some as "premonitions" of the deadly storm, according *El Nuevo Día* newspaper. Some of the children died in the landslide. The drawings were put on exhibit in the Ponce Museum of History.

* * *

It was the day of New Year's Eve, 1986, and, although both New Year's and Christmas were the two days the *San Juan Star* did not publish each year, I was one of the very few journalists on duty at the newspaper—just in case. Just-in-case happened about 3:30 p.m. when a fire broke out at the Dupont Plaza Hotel on Ashford Avenue in Condado. I went to the scene and interviewed survivors, who came out from the hotel's casino gray-faced and coughing, and who anxiously awaited news on the sidewalk outside the hotel about friends and family they were separated from when the fire broke out. Police, firefighters, reporters, cameramen, photographers and onlookers all converged on the scene; people were grim-faced; many cried; a mother was frantically saying that her two daughters were in a room on an upper floor of the hotel; helicopters flew overhead plucking survivors from the roof of the beachfront high-rise. The fire was later ruled an arson set by disgruntled workers in a labor dispute at the hotel. The toll: 97 people dead, 140 injured.

The *Star* put out a special edition for reports on the fire, which I also wrote about for the *Daily News*.

New book Fleshes Out Expanding Clemente Legend

WASHINGTON Joe DiMaggio spent his last years coldly cashing in on his legend. Mickey Mantle damaged his family and himself through his alcoholism before he sought redemption in his last days. Pete Rose, a great baseball player, has shown himself to be much less as human being.

Then there was Roberto Clemente.

"The reality of many athletes, even those who become hailed as deities, is that they diminish with time; Clemente was the opposite, more sure of himself and his large role in life."

That's from a new biography of the great Puerto Rican by David Maraniss, a Pulitzer Prize-winning journalist and editor at *The Washington Post.* Maraniss has written three previous best-sellers: "First in His Class: A biography of Bill Clinton," "When Pride Still Mattered: A Life of Vince Lombardi" and "They Marched into Sunlight: War and Peace, Vietnam and America, October 1967."

Maraniss, a baseball *fanático* from way back—as far back as

the early 1950s, when he first became a Cleveland Indians follower, then, after a family move to Wisconsin, a Milwaukee Braves fan—had taken to Clemente early on. The Pittsburgh Pirates' right fielder became a Maraniss favorite soon after he began his 18-year career in 1955. The idea of a Clemente biography percolated over the years and came to boil in 1999 when Maraniss signed a two-book deal with Simon and Schuster. One book was about Vietnam and America. The second book would be about the Puerto Rican who became the first great Latino baseball star.

Clemente in life, said Maraniss in a recent interview, was a great athlete who was "far from perfect" as a human being. But in his last years, before the plane overloaded with relief supplies for the hurricane victims of Nicaragua went down off Isla Verde on New Year's Eve 1972, the almost always perfect ball player was growing as a person. Now, more than 30 years after his death, Clemente is not looked upon so much with nostalgia to the past, Maraniss writes in the biography. "His myth arcs the other way, to the future, to what people hope they can become."

In death, Roberto Clemente has become "a social force," moving up into the realm of Jackie Robinson, who in 1947 broke the color line as the first black in the Major Leagues. There have been both on-field and off-field parallels between the two, said Maraniss. Like Robinson, Clemente's life has taken on an "extra dimension."

The fans, perhaps, recognize the down-to-earthiness of the ballplayer who grew up near the sugarcane fields of Carolina.

"Clemente was in marked relief to what is going on in baseball today," Maraniss said. "He didn't bulk up [on steroids] for home runs. He didn't have an agent telling him to do good deeds; he did them because of his conscience."

Puerto Ricans have always known about Clemente's humanity, his empathy with children, his kindness and generosity to the poor. But it took mainland Americans a while to understand the man. Stateside sports writers usually covered his on-field heroics adequately as one of the great players of his era—even though Clemente was always complaining that he

never got full credit for his accomplishments. But these same writers also describe some of his feats by resorting to all the clichés in the book about "showboating" Hispanics. In the name of some sort of stupid realistic prose, they quoted him phonetically when he spoke his accented English during interviews.

After one of Clemente's usual heroic performances, this time in the 1961 All-Star Game in San Francisco, when he drove in the winning run in the tenth inning, the *Pittsburgh Post-Gazette's* headline quoted him as saying: "I GET HEET, I FEEL GOOD." Among the sentences in the story: "I say, 'I -ope the Weelhelm (picture Hoyt Willhelm) peetch me outside, so I could hit it to right, but he peetch me inside and I meet it and hit it into right field..."

Maraniss's biography recreates the intensity of the 1960 World Series when the underdog Pirates upset the mighty New York Yankees, highlighted by one of the wildest of seven games, decided in the bottom of the ninth inning by Bill Mazeroski's home run. He re-fires memories of the 1971 World Series when Clemente was probably at his greatest as the Bucs defeated the Baltimore Orioles, again in seven games.

Any baseball fan who saw those games 15 years ago and has not yet reached the Alzheimer's stage, will still vividly remember the fire in Roberto Clemente's bat and arm and heart.

Many in Puerto Rico know the on-field and off-field stories told by Maraniss. An earlier biography by Kal Wagenheim gave a poignant and inspiring account of Clemente's life. The latest book fleshes out the life even further and in the final three chapters, details possibly for the first time, the scary, infuriating story about how the junk heap of a plane was allowed to carry Clemente on his ill-fated, heroic mission to Nicaragua.

Clemente decided to accompany the supplies to make sure they got to the earthquake victims after he angrily learned that provisions sent earlier were being hoarded by the dictatorial regime of Anastasio Somoza.

On page 2 of the biography, Maraniss sums up the many-sided Roberto Clemente noting, "he was agitated, beautiful, sentimental, unsettled, sweet, serious, selfless, haunted, sensitive, contradictory and intensely proud of everything about his native land, including himself."

In the next 350 pages, the author gives ample, dramatic, stirring evidence of that description of a human being as imperfect as the next man, but also as sainted as few others.

April 17, 2006

Roberto Clemente

'Black Smoke Filled the Casino'

"They were still dealing the cards when the smoke started pouring though the casino. The blackjack dealer said there was nothing to worry about." But less than 10 seconds later, the casino at the Dupont Plaza Hotel turned into a scene of incredible chaos and panic, said Tom Cadden, 35, a lawyer from Meriden, Conn.

"Black smoke filled the casino," he said. "I picked up a chair and threw it through a plate-glass window and jumped out onto a wooden ledge about 15 feet down. Ten other people followed me and the ledge collapsed, and we tumbled down onto bodies and broken glass."

Cadden spoke while sitting on a beach lounger used as a make-shift stretcher on a side street outside the hotel. His pants legs were covered with blood and his left foot appeared broken. He was waiting for an ambulance to take him to a hospital.

Jeremy Citron, 27, of Miami, was also in the casino when the fire broke out. "Thick black smoke poured across the top of the ceiling and there were several explosions of glass. People panicked as they rushed to the door. There were a lot of elderly people in there, and only one exit door," Citron said.

The door led into a lobby choked with black smoke, he said. He also got out through a window smashed by a croupier. "I tried to help as many people as I could. Oh God, it was terrible. I'm so lucky to be alive," he said, sobbing.

He estimated there were 300 to 400 people in the casino when the fire broke out.

Several of the survivors said they noticed no sprinkler system working in the hotel and heard no alarm sound during the blaze. Although the fire appeared to be confined to the first two floors, smoke poured though the corridors all the way up to the 18th floor, and seeped through the vents in the emergency fire staircase, survivors said.

Jan. 1, 1987

Smoke pours from the Dupont Plaza Hotel in a fire that took 97 lives. The fire was set by disgruntled hotel employees, four of whom were charged with and convicted of arson and murder. (José Ismael Fernández/Archivo Histórico *El Nuevo Día*)

500 Feared Dead in Puerto Rico Mudslide

Ponce, P.R.—The world of Barrio Mameyes came to an end with an ear-splitting thunderclap while its inhabitants slept.

A mountain soaked by two days of torrential rain turned into a mudslide that officials now fear claimed more than 500 lives.

Broken homes lie like trampled matchboxes at the foot of the verdant hills rimming the northern section of this south coast city, the island's second largest.

Twisted zinc roofs and broken doors are scattered, as are a Barbie doll with one leg broken off and records by Latin singing stars Vincentico Valdez and Marco Antonio Muñiz. The title of one of the records—"La Ultima Noche" (The Last Night).

Edwin Reyes said that among those lost were his wife's parents.

"My wife is in a shelter with my 4-year-old daughter," Reyes said. "She's pregnant. I haven't had the heart to tell her yet, about her mother and father."

Down by the ravine, where the rain formed a pool 50 feet deep, a distressed rescue worker lamented, "We're hooking them out as though they were fish."

Oct. 10, 1985

Homes are destroyed by mudslide in Barrio Mamayes,
where the death toll has been put at 129 to 300 residents.
(José Ismael Fernández/Archivo Histórico *El Nuevo Día*)

Greatest Wallenda Falls to Death

San Juan—Karl Wallenda, 73, the patriarch of the greatest high-wire family in circus history, was caught in a gust of wind while walking across a cable strung between two tall building yesterday and plunged 120 feet to his death.

Wallenda lost his balance during a publicity appearance, made a heart-stopping grab for the wire, missed, and fell through the air, still holding tight to his long balancing pole.

The tough old aerialist struck the roof of a taxicab parked in a hotel driveway, then landed on the pavement. Witnesses rushed to his aid, but Wallenda was lifeless. An ambulance took him to Presbyterian Hospital, where doctors worked to revive him. He was pronounced dead a few minutes later.

Wallenda, the founder and leader of the Great Wallendas, was walking across 300 feet of cable suspended between the oceanfront Condado Holiday Inn and the hotel's Laguna Wing annex in a promotional appearance for the Pan American Circus. He was appearing nightly at the circus, in a tent outside the Roberto Clemente Coliseum, with his 17-year-old granddaughter, Rietta, who was in the crowd, yesterday when Wallenda fell.

Wallenda was about two-thirds of the way across the wire when he began to kneel to secure his footing. Suddenly a gust of wind blew in off the ocean and threw him off balance. Without letting go of his balancing pole, he frantically tried to grab the cable with one hand, but missed it and tumbled off with the pole still clutched in both hands.

About 250 horror-struck spectators, many of them tourists, saw the plunge. It took place on Ashford Avenue, the main thoroughfare in the Condado tourist section of San Juan.

Wallenda, a high-wire performer, since his youth, had to lean into a strong wind even as he began the stunt. Because the hotel is taller than the annex, he also had to walk up a steep incline.

"Right from the start he seemed to be having trouble with the wind," said one witness, Pipo Grajales, who was watching from a room in the hotel. "He kept yelling to the people below to tighten the guidelines."

Grajales said that help in pulling on the guidelines was provided by some passersby who were called into service on the spot.

Wallenda began his walk at about 11:05 a.m. about eight minutes later, he fell.

Another witness, Victor Abboud, an accountant from Montreal, said. "I saw him go down on his knees on the wire and I thought he was kneeling to rest. But then I saw he was shaking. The wind blew him off and he want all the way down, head first."

March 28, 1978

Karl Wallenda, moments before he fell to his death from the high-wire between the upper floors of two hotels in the Condado section of San Juan (José Ismael Fernández/Archivo Histórico *El Nuevo Día*)

Terrorism

*C*ombine violent crime with uncompromising politics and what you have is a terrorism that strikes on all fanatical ends of the spectrum. While the FALN was blowing up stateside taverns and government and business facilities in New York and Chicago in the name of Puerto Rico independence, *Los Macheteros* were killing U.S. sailors and destroying military planes on the island, also in the name of a politically independent Puerto Rico. Neither group explained just how "independent" the island would be when ruled by the Marxist-Leninist government they espoused. Several U.S. business and government offices were also bombed around the island in the late 1970s and the 1980s.

Among other acts, the FALN *(Fuerzas Armadas de Liberación Nacional)* was linked to the bombing in 1975 of the historic Fraunces Tavern in New York's Wall Street district, which killed four and injured 43 persons. *Los Macheteros* (the Machete Wielders) got national attention when one of its alleged members, Victor Gerena, a Wells Fargo guard, robbed $7 million from the bank's depot in Hartford, Conn. It was the largest cash robbery in U.S. history at the time. Gerena supposedly turned over some of the loot to *Los Macheteros* to be used in their activities for island independence, and took off for Cuba, where he reportedly still lives.

In 1999, President Bill Clinton offered clemency to 16 imprisoned FALN members. The only one who refused the pardon was Oscar López Rivera. López Rivera, born in 1943, was sentenced in 1981 to 55 years for seditious conspiracy, use of force to commit robbery, interstate transportation of firearms and conspiracy to transport explosives with intent to destroy government property. In 1988 he was given an additional 15 years for conspiring to escape from prison. A strong campaign by political, religious and other leaders, both on the island and in the states, was waged to free López Rivera from prison. Among others, Vermont Senator Bernie Sanders tweeted in 2016 while campaigning for the Democratic Party presidential candidacy, "Oscar López Rivera has served 34 years in prison for his commitment to Puerto Rico's independence. I say to President Obama: let him out." López Rivera was given his freedom by President Obama in January,2017.

Down through the years individual members of the Macheteros and the FALN have been arrested and given prison terms. The two groups currently are dormant.

Then there were extreme right-wing Cuban exiles who many have accused of carrying out two especially heinous crimes on the island. One was the murder in 1979 of Carlos Muñiz Varela, a young Cuban-born travel agent who grew up in Puerto Rico and whose horrendous sin, in the eyes of the killer, or killers, was arranging visits for tourists, and others, to the island of his birth. The other was the killing, in 1976, of Santiago "Chagui" Mari Pesquera, who was the son of Puerto Rican Socialist Party Leader Juan Mari Bras. The killers were never brought to justice in either case.

In 1977, Allan Randall, a corporation lawyer who represented companies in cases involving unions, was shot to death in the basement garage of his condominium home in Condado. The killers described themselves as "labor commandos." The following articles give further details on the killings of the Navy men and the assassination of Randall.

P.R. Gunmen Kill 2 U.S. Navy Men

San Juan, P.R.—Pro-independence terrorists boarded a bus carrying Navy personnel to work yesterday morning and turned it into a scene of bloody carnage, killing two Navy men and wounding 10 others, including three women.

Three terrorist groups, saying that they were at war with "Yankee imperialists," claimed joint responsibility in a communique for the ambush. They said that the attack was in retaliation for the death of one of their followers in a federal prison last month.

The communique said that the attack was the work of the "joint forces" of the Volunteers for the Puerto Rican Revolution, the Boricua Popular Army (also known as the Macheteros) and the Armed Forces of Popular Resistance.

"We warn the Yankee imperialists that they must respect the life and the security of our prisoners according to the Geneva convention on war," the communique said.

Rear Adm. Arthur K. Knoizen, senior U.S. naval officer in the Caribbean, called the attack a "heinous crime that we cannot tolerate."

The ambush occurred at 6:20 a.m. as personnel were being transported in a yellow bus from a naval communications facility in Toa Baja, 10 miles west of San Juan, to work at the Sabana Seca Naval radar station on the island's north coast.

The bus was cut off by a white van outside the station. About four gunmen jumped from the van, forced their way onto the bus and sprayed more than 40 bullets into the vehicle, killing the bus driver and a radio technician.

Authorities here said the attackers opened fire with a heavy-gauge shotgun and pistols.

One of the survivors said that the driver was killed immediately when he was shot under the right eye. One of the passengers grabbed the wheel, spun the bus around and drove it back to the Sabana Seca communications facility, the survivor said.

The Navy would not release the names of the dead or wounded until relatives had been notified.

Last month, Angel Rodríguez Cristóbal, sent after his trial to federal prison in Tallahassee, Fla., was found hanged in his cell. Prison authorities said he had committed suicide but radical independence groups claim that he was slain in a CIA plot.

The Navy has come under attack for using Vieques, an offshore island, as a target-practice site. Recently, 21 protesters were tried in federal court here for demonstrating against bombing maneuvers. Several persons were jailed.

Terrorist attacks on the island in the recent past base usually involved late night bombings of federal facilities and large U.S. business concerns.

Last month, simultaneous bombs went off at a Coast Guard installation and the U.S. Customs House in San Juan and at a federal building in Chicago. The Puerto Rican radical group FALN took responsibility for those bombings.

Yesterday's deaths were the first involving U.S. military personnel here since 1970, when a serviceman was gunned down by terrorists seeking revenge for the death of a student during riots at the University of Puerto Rico.

Dec. 4, 1987

Alan Randall and the Cool Killers Among Us

"There are crimes of passion and crimes of logic. The boundary between them is not clearly defined. But the Penal Code makes the convenient distinction of premeditation. We are living in the era of premeditation and the perfect crime. Our criminals are no longer helpless children who would plead love as their excuse. On the contrary, they are adults and they have a perfect alibi: philosophy, which can be used for any purpose—even for transforming murderers into judges."

Albert Camus

The cool killers are among us. They no longer murder out of passion for revenge or for hatred or for what they see as the immediate solution to an intolerable injustice. Murder for them is no more than a "revolutionary tactic," an act to be committed after "a process of investigation and analysis," an adjunct to the "historical moment," a logical deduction justified by doctrine and philosophy.

The cool, logical killers who have entered the underside of Puerto Rican life for the first time are the group of "labor commandos" who have taken credit for the murder of attorney Alan Randall. This newspaper received through the mail the other day a 2,200-word document from them that attempts to justify their killing of Randall in detached, almost scholarly, modern-day Marxist-Leninist terms, faultlessly phrased by a person, or persons, of obvious intelligence. The document describes Randall as "a soldier who fell in the combat" of class warfare. It charges him once again with being a CIA agent and with participating in "a repressive antilabor drive. . ." and as being a "personal participant" in a supposed U.S. intelligence plan to combat labor gains on the island. Nowhere is sufficient proof given of the charges.

The document speaks of the use of "revolutionary violence" as a "means within the context of a political process," of "global struggle," of using "the means and forms of struggle most effective in each historical moment." It insists that the execution of Randall was not a political assassination or a criminal act, but a "revolutionary tactic" sanctioned, in essence, by revolutionary history.

Thus, in the supposed revolutionary struggle for a better, more humane world, Alan Randall was objectified for "investigation and analysis" and found through this dispassionate process guilty and sentenced by these philosophic judges to die, his death receiving authorization by their interpretation of history. The sentence was presumably carried out with the same cold-blooded detachment as it was passed.

Randall was murdered with the same "objective" inhumanity as murders carried out by totalitarian governments against subjects deemed unworthy of life. The totalitarian state usually goes to great lengths to justify its condemnations. Its victims almost always are charged with committing crimes not against other individuals, but against an amorphous mass called "the state" or "the people"—just as Randall was accused of crimes against the "working class." It is as if the "labor commandos" have set themselves up as a provisional government and as such have assumed the right to make judgments of life and death. Only the totalitarian mentality assumes the complete freedom to these judgments. The irony, of course, is that these alleged revolutionaries would say that totalitarian governments are their mortal enemies.

Reading this eight-page political thesis gives one the chilling feeling that the greater the rational for murder, the more insane the act is. It is insane because the murderer believes there is a logical basis for an act that is futile in both the philosophical and the practical sense. If the supposed goal of the revolution is a more just and moral world, then how can an act of injustice and immorality—to trivialize the life of another human being by reducing the ultimate judgment on that life to a "revolutionary tactic"—how can this mental derangement of the thought process bring about a more principled world?

Even if Alan Randall were all the things his purported killers accuse him of being, even if he too were caught up in the general madness that has produced both a CIA and terrorist labor commandos, how does his death change anything on a practical level in the "revolutionary struggle"? Is the millennium any closer because Alan Randall was murdered? Only the mentally deranged would think so.

What Alan Randall's murder has done is to separate his killers from the true goals of the working class and of human brotherhood. It has separated them from the community of people who refuse to legitimize murder for any cause. And in the end, if any moments of real clarity come to these thinking beings, it should separate them from their deeper selves for adding to the general injustice in the world.

Nov. 1, 1985

Double Whammy

*T*he 1960s and 1970s were comparatively good economic times for Puerto Rico. Still, just about one out of every two Puerto Ricans was considered living below the federal poverty level. Help came in the way of aid from the federal government: the food stamp program was fully extended to the island in the early Seventies, and federal funds rose into the billions of dollars annually.

Section 936 of the federal tax code was put into effect in 1976. Through the new provision, U.S. corporations were given significant incentives to locate subsidiaries on the island, in the hope they would create many more jobs, even though little or no taxes would accrue to the U.S. or Commonwealth treasuries.

When Section 936 was in effect, U.S. corporations benefited greatly. Some say the companies made out like bandits by, among other ways, claiming profits from the island subsidiaries that were really made by their stateside enterprises, thus eliminating further tax payments to the U.S. Treasury. Nevertheless, because of these generous tax incentives for business, Puerto Rico's economy improved as the island developed a substantial manufacturing sector.

The petrochemical industry was also producing jobs and revenues for the island. Commonwealth officials had envisioned a vast network of petrochemical plants processing crude oil into synthetic materials and finished products—and creating tens of thousands of jobs. Then came the 1973 Arab-Israeli war and its aftermath when Arab states decided to cut oil production, sending the price of oil needed by the petrochemical plants skyrocketing. Firms such as Corco (Commonwealth Oil Refining Company), PPG Industries and Union Carbide closed shop on the island. The closings caused huge economic and social problems for once relatively well-off small island towns where the plants were located.

Then, in the 1980s, came the administration of President Ronald Reagan. While 936 remained on the books (the program was eliminated by the Clinton administration in 1995 after being deemed "corporate welfare"), Reaganomics meant, among other things, a new, reduced food aid program for the island. Puerto Rico was given a yearly block grant through the Nutrition Assistance Program (NAP) and the recipients received checks instead of food stamps. This resulted in $200 million less in food aid annually. Other federal aid programs were cut by another $200-$400 million. The official island jobless rate, at about 10 percent in the Seventies, more than doubled in the early Eighties. The Caribbean Basin Initiative, created in 1983, eliminated the island's unique position in the region of offering investors a special trading relationship and tax advantages with the United States. The CBI offered more or less the same investment incentives and tax breaks to competitors in the region.

If one were to judge by visiting the tourist areas of San Juan and the gated, middle-class suburbs—as well as Plaza las Américas, which opened in 1969 and became the largest shopping mall in the Caribbean—the economy still seemed to be doing fine. But trips out on the island and to the slum areas of the city were more discouraging; the able-bodied and the young there stopped looking for jobs. The following story gives some idea of the cost of Reaganomics for Puerto Rico.

Reaganomics Hits Puerto Rico Hard

San Juan, P.R.—When the United States sneezes, Puerto Rico gets pneumonia. And now that the U.S. economy is wheezing hard, the island may soon be ready for the oxygen tent.

Because Puerto Rico is so heavily tied to the U.S. economy, because the income of the average Puerto Rican family income is one third that of an average stateside family and because the cost of living here is higher, the combination of recession and Reaganomics is beginning to lay the island low.

Puerto Rico's economy is in big trouble, and things are expected to get worse—much, much worse if the Reagan administration continues certain policies.

Puerto Rico's official unemployment rate has reached 21.6%. Economists predict that by the end of the year one of every four persons looking for a job here will fail. That is not counting the tens of thousands among the island's 3.2 million inhabitants who have given up hope of finding a job.

Jobs are disappearing, as U.S. subsidiaries cut back and hundreds of public service employees, who make up more than 30% of the work force, are laid off and their jobs eliminated. Thousands more have had their workweeks and paychecks reduced—some by as much as half.

The Puerto Rican government is struggling with federal cuts and an estimated $100 million less in revenues. A Puerto Rican law requires the government to operate on a balanced budget.

Tourism, the island's third largest industry, appears to be holding its own.

The Reagan budget cuts are expected to wreak special havoc here. The island is losing $400 million in federal funds, including $300 million in food stamps which go to 60 percent of the population.

Puerto Rico, as a Commonwealth, shares equally with the states in numerous federal welfare programs. In the latest fiscal year, the island received more than $4 billion in federal aid, and more than $1 billion in food stamps.

In July, Puerto Rico will be receiving food-stamp aid in block grants, which will reduce its share by 25 percent. None of the 50 states is being given this treatment. The Reagan Administration has said that Puerto Rico, which pays no federal taxes, has been getting too large a share of the program.

While many observers agree that the island has become too dependent on federal aid in general, and food stamps in particular, they see the Reagan Administration's weaning process as providing too little, too soon, without offering adequate alternatives.

Business bankruptcies are up 80 percent from last year, setting a record. And a record number of personal bankruptcies also have been filed.

The island's efforts to bring US factories here, once the main thrust of the Operation Bootstrap economic recovery program that transferred Puerto Rico from the "poorhouse of the Caribbean" – as social scientists once called it – to a relatively prospering society, have been stymied. This is the result, among other things, of a federal attempt to change the local tax-incentives law.

Many U.S. companies have been shifting stateside profits to tax-free Puerto Rican subsidiaries. The Internal Revenue Service wants to stop this tax dodge by collecting a "tollgate" tax on profits sent from the island to the mainland. The law now allows these profits to be repatriated tax-free. Stateside companies have put on hold plans to setup shop here pending the outcome of the IRS effort.

The Reagan Administration's developing Caribbean-basin plan could further damage the island's economy. The plan, being touted as the most important U.S. aid effort in the hemisphere since the Alliance for Progress, is aimed at preventing the region from going Communist.

The proposal calls for reducing or removing U.S. tariffs on Caribbean products. This would wipe out the competitive price advantage of Puerto Rican rum in the states. Since excise taxes on mainland rum sales also revert to the island, this could cut deeply into a much-needed revenue source which amounted to $250 million last year.

The plan also will offer U.S. businesses incentives to invest in other Caribbean islands, which could undo Operation Bootstrap even further.

The U.S. once proudly paraded Puerto Rico

before developing nations as "the Showcase of Democracy."

"This is what you can do if you stick with us," said Washington of the island's booming economy in the 1950s and 1960s.

The boom is now rapidly turning to bust. What price anti-communism in the Caribbean if it means 3 million Americans again in the poorhouse they struggled so hard to escape?

Jan. 24, 1982

The Washington-
San Juan Nexus

"*A* billion here, a billion there, and pretty soon you're talking real money." Illinois Sen. Everett Dirksen supposedly said that about the federal budget in the 1960s. (He insisted he had been misquoted.) Nevertheless, it is a quote that could have been offered vis-a-vis federal funds to Puerto Rico over the years.

In 1970, the island received $727 million from Washington. That was before the food stamp program went into effect. By 1989 that figure was up to $6 billion, according to the Commonwealth Planning Board. (The funding from Washington then kept soaring to $23.5 billion in 2011, according to the Consolidated Federal Funds Report. The Census Bureau stopped making the report public in 2012.)

While the funds did help keep Puerto Ricans out of extreme poverty during those years, a significant share came from earned benefits for veterans and from federal benefits that Puerto Ricans paid into, such as Medicare and Social Security. And it didn't, and still doesn't, hurt U.S. businesses to keep Puerto Rico economically afloat—to a degree— since the U.S. is by far Puerto Rico's main trading partner, and the hefty food aid program to the island goes back to the U.S. farmers who produce most of the food the island residents consume.

There was plenty of lobbying in the 1960s-1980s for increased federal transfers, not only by the Puerto Rican government, whose officials appeared to treat Washington as a second home, but also by U.S. corporate interests, whose companies were making many millions of tax-free dollars in their Puerto Rico operations.

And, of course, politics came into very large play during those years. For one, the Cold War was still chilling international relations and the U.S. wanted to show that Castro and Cuba did not have the answer for the economic and political woes in the Caribbean. Look to (a propped up) Puerto Rico and the benefits of capitalism for a better life in the hemisphere, was the message from Washington, and for which many of the dollars to San Juan flowed.

Then, in those years, the presidential candidates started noting that Puerto Rico would be a good place to visit, not only for sun, sand and sea, but for actual votes. Presidential primaries began on the island in 1980, the winner taking all of Puerto Rico's votes at the national conventions. (While island residents, who have been U.S. citizens since 1917, still do not have the presidential vote, Puerto Rico gets to cast 60 votes at the Democratic convention and 23 votes at the Republican get-together.) The candidates also took note that island residents could influence the vote of their stateside brethren and that there was enough big bucks in Puerto Rico to hold fundraisers there. The island fundraisers also became popular with members of Congress. The all-time congressional visitor in those years was Democratic Rep. Charles Rangel, whose bailiwick included East Harlem, or *El Barrio*, as it became known. Rangel was a frequent island money-raiser. He claimed he couldn't care less about the island's political status and was very concerned about improving the everyday life of his Puerto Rican constituents. Many congressional Republicans became sudden statehood advocates in their fund-raising visits.

Among those active vis-a-vis Puerto Rico during those years were both the Kennedy and the Bush clans. It all began when President John Kennedy and First Lady Jacqueline Kennedy spent Dec. 15-16, 1962 in Puerto Rico with full media coverage of their wildly enthusiastic welcome by the population. The visit followed a White House reception in November 1961 for then-Puerto Rico Gov. Luis Muñoz Marín and exiled Spanish cellist Pablo Casals, who called Puerto Rico home. The Kennedy-Muñoz connection extended down through the years to the national Democratic Party and the island's Popular Democratic Party. Officials and candidates from each party backed the other via visits and fundraisers, both in the states and on the island. The Kennedy clan—Robert, Ted, Jackie—made several Puerto Rico visits in the 1960s to the 1980s.

The Bush family, meanwhile, connected to the island's statehood movement, and the New Progressive Party. (The NPP was firmly in the Republican wing until the late 1970s when some of its leaders, including then-Gov. Carlos Romero Barceló, became allied with the national Democrats.) Then-Vice President George H.W. Bush came to Puerto Rico in 1988 in his run for the Republican presidential nomination. He won Puerto Rico's GOP plebiscite after touring the island and insisting over and over on "Statehood. *Ahora*!" (Statehood. Now!) Bush brought up the island's status in his Feb. 1989 State of the Union, noting that "personally I strongly favor statehood." (Former Florida Gov. Jeb Bush kept the family's ties with the statehood movement over the years on island visits, though former-President George W. Bush showed less enthusiasm for any change in the island's status.)

Here is a story of an island visit in 1980 by Jacqueline Kennedy on behalf of brother-in-law Ted Kennedy's White House challenge to sitting President Jimmy Carter.

Rep. Charles Rangel, D-N.Y., rides down Fifth
Avenue in the 2014 Puerto Rican Day parade.

Jackie in San Juan Rides Tide of Vivas!

San Juan, P.R.—Jacqueline Kennedy Onassis rode a tidal wave of Puerto Rican enthusiasm yesterday as she hit the campaign trail here for her former brother-in-law, Sen. Edward M. Kennedy of Massachusetts.

Puerto Rico will hold its first Democratic presidential primary in history on Sunday; Kennedy, President Carter and Gov. Edmund G. Brown Jr. of California are on the ballot. At stake are 41 votes at the Democratic National Convention, which will nominate the party's presidential candidate.

Onassis, widow of President John F. Kennedy and Aristotle Onassis, the Greek shipping tycoon, was mobbed yesterday by several thousand persons when she visited the Plaza las Américas shopping center in Hato Rey. She shook hands, kissed people and was kissed back. She was cheered with choruses of "Kennedy, Ken-nedy!" She stopped traffic as she walked through the narrow streets of Old San Juan and drew a crowd of hundreds. She also visited the seaside slum of La Perla.

Earlier in the day, Onassis had given a short speech in Spanish to about 800 cheering women who paid $20 each for breakfast with the former First Lady. Monday night, she raised $50,000 for Kennedy's campaign at a $250 a ticket cocktail party. Before that, she visited a school for retarded children and, in the school cafeteria, sampled such Puerto Rican dishes as *bacalaito frito* (fried codfish cake) and *sorullo* (cornmeal fritter).

Veteran observers could not remember Mrs. Onassis being so outgoing in any political campaign. She spoke freely with reporters and seemed genuinely buoyed by the overwhelming reception.

She said she continue campaigning for Kennedy, but has "no plans" to go to Illinois, which will hold its primary Tuesday.

"Nothing could be as nice as campaigning in Puerto Rico," she said she would continue campaigning. "I've never seen such a show of affection anyplace."

March 11, 1980

Jackie Kennedy with local journalists, including Friedman, right, and politicians as she campaigns in Old San Juan for brother-in-law Edward Kennedy. (*Star* photo by Eddie Crespo.)

Show Business

The entertainment scene on the island in the Sixties, Seventies and Eighties was certainly jumping. Local television shows featured comedian José Miguel Agrelot, singer-band leader Tito Rodríguez, body-shaker Iris Chacón, El Gran Combo salsa band; in night spots around town, like Ocho Puertas in Old San Juan, such local performers as Danny Rivera, Lucecita Benítez, Chucho Avellanet, Ednita Nazario and Nydia Caro took off to stardom and were booked into the big nightclubs in the tourist hotels in Condado and Isla Verde. Headlining at those hotels were, among many, many others, Sammy Davis Jr., Liza Minnelli, Tony Bennett, James Brown, The Supremes, The Temptations, Ella Fitzgerald, Tom Jones, Jerry Lewis, Johnny Matthis, Tito Puente, La Lupe, Celia Cruz, Marco Antonio Muñiz, José Feliciano. The ballparks filled with concerts by Raphael from Spain and Rubén Blades from Panama. Island theaters featured a young Raul Julia in *Bye Birdie* and Oscar-winning great José Ferrer doing a reprise of his role on Broadway as Don Quixote in *Man of La Mancha.* Ferrer, of Cyrano de Bergerac and Toulouse-Lautrec movie fame, also performed a song-and-dance act at the Sheraton Hotel in Condado.

Hollywood visited Puerto Rico in those years. Woody Allen used the island for *Bananas*, his manic take-off on a Caribbean revolution, which featured lots of local actors, including Jacobo Morales and Miguel Angel Suarez. Local scenes were also shot for "Show of Force," a movie based on the Cerro Maravilla killings, starring Robert Duvall, Kevin Spacey and Andy Garcia. The above mentioned Jacobo Morales, who also directed films, had his 1989 movie, <u>Lo que le pasó a Santiago</u> (*What Happened to Santiago*) nominated for an Academy Award for Best Foreign Film, a first for a Puerto Rican movie. An actor by the name of Cary Grant also made a brief visit to the island. (See story below.)

An addendum to Hollywood's adventures on the island: In the late 1960s, the director Elia Kazan and the writer Budd Schulberg (both of whom had won Academy Awards for *On the Waterfront*) were in and out of Puerto Rico several months as they prepared for their next film, *In the Streets*, about one Puerto Rican family's journey from an island mountain town to the San Juan slums to New York. Kazan and Schulberg interviewed local actors, contacted Fomento to set up a local company, took trips around the island and visited San Juan restaurants and night spots. The two Hollywood honchos talked about making more than one movie in Puerto Rico. They mulled setting a story from the Greek classical comedy *Lysistrata* on Culebra or Vieques—both the scenes of military exercises at the time—in which the female population vows to withhold what the opposite sex wants most until the Navy calls it quits on the island.

None of the films ever got made.

In 2009, shortly before his death, Schulberg, writing in *The Guardian* newspaper about his friendship with Kazan, recalled those efforts:

"For the Puerto Rican film, *In the Streets*, which our producer Sam Spiegel pulled out of and was never made, we spent three months in Puerto Rico doing research. It was more than research. Very much hands on. We scoured Puerto Rican Harlem together. We had the Puerto Rican hero light heavyweight champ, the late José Torres, as our guide. We became so immersed that we were thinking in Puerto Rican. When Spiegel imperiously decided that 'the public would not be interested in a lot of poor Puerto Ricans,' we were devastated. We had come to love these people..."

The following stories include an article about the never-made movie, an interview- review of José Ferrer's show biz talents, an interview-review with Sammy Davis Jr., a Carey Grant adieu interview, a quick lesson in jazz history by the great jazz trumpeter "Dizzy" Gillespie, who appeared at a local hotel and gave island concerts for UPR and Sacred Heart University students. And, not to be omitted, the Las Vegas influence on the larger, more expensive tourist resorts, most especially the one-and-only El San Juan Hotel during its show biz heyday.

City Side

How would he make his entrance—swaggering through the audience as Cyrano de Bergerac with Pinocchio nose and unsheathed sword, sweeping out a sardonic, plumed-hat bow? Hobbling through, a knee-high Toulouse-Lautrec only the top of his bowler skimming visibly above the tables, laboriously, painfully, yet with defiant, head-shaking pride, caning his way to the center of the stage?

Hell no! It's José "show biz" Ferrer trotting through the opening night crowd, bounding on stage and welcoming one and all with an upbeat, special lyrics opener to the tune of "Cabaret."

That's the way he opened Monday night at the Sheraton Hotel's Salon Carnaval and when he closed an hour and a quarter later with "Every Time We Say Goodbye" ("I die a little"). Hundreds cheered. Local boy, in his first on-stage appearance back in his own back yard (he was born and partially bred in Miramar), made nothing but good.

So now that he has proved himself a success in the theater, in films (an Academy Award for acting, *Cyrano*, 1951), on television, as an actor, writer, director, producer, singer, dancer, comedian, what's left? Where will his quest lead him next? What other fields are left for him to conquer?

"I'm not trying to conquer anything," José Ferrer answered adamantly. "I'm just trying to earn a living. So, many people think I'm on an expedition to conquer. I just want to make a decent living so that I can feed my children" (five of whom—by former spouse Rosemary Clooney—are accompanying their bearded father here during his two-week engagement).

"A quest is the last thing in the world that I'm on. My only quest is to develop myself to my full potential, whether it is as an actor, director or nightclub performer. The people who foot the bill are entitled to the best you can give them. You give them their money's worth and they give you their money. I'm just trying to make enough money as pleasantly as possible."

The 56-year-old performer spent the first six years of his

101

life in Puerto Rico, then returned every other year until he entered Princeton University, where he studied architecture and earned his Bachelor of Arts degree in 1933. After a 16-year pause ("Once I started acting, I was afraid to leave the phone for five minutes"), he has returned intermittently to the island and now says, "I wish I could live here. I love the climate. The temperature of the air is unique. You can't find it anywhere else in the world."

But would he be HOME: Is Puerto Rico his home, does he feel truly Puerto Rican?

"A person like me has many homes. New York is home, so is California, London, Paris, Rome and certainly Puerto Rico. I've lived in all these places. But I still do feel very Latin in my background and culture, and very Puerto Rican. I also feel very American."

Returning to opening night, Ferrer said this was the best night club audience so far. He had previously brought the cabaret act to Hollywood (Florida), Montreal and Melbourne, Australia. "I never enjoyed working in a night club as much as I did last night. After an hour and fifteen minutes I didn't feel any fatigue. The audience was

so warm and receptive. It was really an experience."

Yes, it was, fifteen songs, a little dancing, jokes, some recitation to introduce and thread together three songs from "Man of la Mancha," in which Ferrer has appeared in the past and will appear again starting Sept. 23 for a one-year road tour. You may think he would come across, person-to-person, (the Sheraton's supper club is one of the most intimate in town, assuring—demanding—a personal relationship between performer and audience) a bit stentoriously, a declaimer of song and prose. Not so, up there, pressed between the audience on three sides and the swinging sounds of the excellent Charlie Rodríguez orchestra wailing on top-notch arrangements behind him. Ferrer comes across—warmly ("What a Difference a Day Makes"—in Spanish and English), wryly ("The Snake"), movingly ("Maman," the "La Mancha" mediev). Walter Hurston-wistfully "Autumn Leaves," "This is all I Ask")) and a combination of all the above in a wonderful number. "The Song and Dance Man."

Ferrer proves once again that a great voice is no prerequisite for putting over a song in a night club. Instead, you gotta have—heart, soul, savvy and a little bit of schmaltz. He combines all these on "The Song and Dance Man" and on "Maman," a Charles Aznavour-like chant about a French soldier writing home before his first kill. One number, "The Men in a Little Girl's Life," is a bit too thick on the latter ingredient for my taste.

Aside from this, the show builds beautifully and about halfway through Ferrer bits top stride and continues to bound along and display still one more side of his talented self—the one that is light on 'dramatics,' and heavy on *simpatico*.

Aug. 29, 1968

José Ferrer as Cyrano de Bergerac

City Side

While leading the reporter to his suite for the interview, Sammy Davis Jr., told a hotel employee: "Ask the cats to send up some ice." The employee looked confused "Cats? Cats? Ice for the cats?" Davis reeled off toward a wall in silent hysterics. But from then on, he was rapping in his new bag articulately and fervently, though not without humor, about Black and White – together, apart, against one another. It started when he was asked if he still believes, as he was quoted in the *New York Times* as believing, that the Negro artist in America will never be accepted entirely on his own.

Yes, he still believes so. "You still hear someone called a Negro football player, a Negro actor. No one speaks of Kirk Douglas as a Jewish actor. I live for the day when Negros will just be actors and actresses, not Black actors and Black actresses. Sidney Poitier has proved that you don't need these labels. He's the number one box office actor. Not the number one colored actor. These labels are just one of hundreds of things we unconsciously do in our society to give the hot heads a little edge."

The hot heads, don't necessarily come in one particular nationality or color. "It seems that most men are losing the art of reasoning. The days of sitting down and discussing problems on a calm, honest level are quickly disappearing. It's frightening. And it's not just Black and White. It's Black against Black, White against White, Japanese students against their government, French students against theirs. And racism isn't just an American problem. They have a race problem in Great Britain that's second to none. They only reason they're not burning down buildings there yet is that Blacks are about 10 to 15 years behind. They are still using the protest methods of Martin Luther King. But they're advancing, every month is like a year for them. If nothing concrete is done there, as long as men in Enoch Powell (a Member of Parliament) can make statements in the House of Commons as he does against- not only Blacks, but against Indians, Pakistanis and all foreigners, then the buildings will start burning in Great Britain also."

What about those Blacks in America who say that the only way Negros can be given an equal chance is by tearing down, then restructuring the present society? "If society has to be torn down to face the problems of today, then, I'm all for it – if something constructive can come out of it. But I don't think the Blacks in America are ready for a total commitment to violence or toward a total revolution. I don't think it's our way. We're not about to go to the hills to fight a revolution against the government."

"I consider myself a militant, in a way. But militancy has many faces. I don't see how we can fight a physical revolution. I believe in standing up for your individual dignity and telling the man we want what's written on that piece of paper. Give me that equal start. But beyond that, we damn well better work for anything else we get. With all its faults, America is still the greatest country in the world."

But one of these faults is portraying many Black militants as some kind of monsters. Davis spoke of the subterfuge he had to use to get Ron Karanga, a Black militant, on the Johnny Carson TV show, which he was emceeing for the evening. He said the television executives at first did not want Karanga on the show, until Davis told them, "When he comes on the show, I'm gonna give it to him." They replied, Davis said: "That's it, Sam. Good idea."

Karanga came on the show and Davis sat back and let him do his thing, which was speaking about giving Black pride to Black people. That's what he teaches, "Say it loud, I'm Black and I'm proud." That's so damn positive. He's telling this to the guy in the street who doesn't have any pride. That's what so much of it is all about. That's why college kids take over school buildings and say, "We want Black history: if you don't give it to us, we won't give you back your building.' Can you imagine what guts it takes for a group of Black kids to do something like that? When I was a kid, I was told to be nice and polite and keep my place in school and that's all."

Well, what about the Black group which has been known to "keep its place" less than any other: the Black Panthers? How does he feel about them?

"I know what the Black Panthers are talking about. And I agree with them. The only thing, I don't want to see a lot of Black leaders dead in the streets. I can put on a black leather jacket and go out in the street with a machine gun, but it don't do no good if I get killed. You must do something constructive. And I don't mean the Urban League or the NAACP. Not that they don't perform good services. It's always the lawyers from these groups who are defending the militants in court. "

"But someone has to stand in the middle. If all the leaders get killed, who is going to build that Black society they're always talking about? I can get up on the stage and yell Black Power all night. But it doesn't do any good. You've got to act constructively."

"What we've got to do is show the government we can move as a force. If there was a way to say that all Black people who hold jobs ain't going to work on Wednesday and you did it – then you'd be proving you can move as a force; you have an are to move in, sensibly.

You can threaten large economic boycotts unless certain things are done. But we're still 10 years away from that. "

Davis believes that if Robert Kennedy had lived, he would have been elected President and "attacked honestly all the immediate racial problems. Bobby Kennedy knew the problems of the Black ghetto as far as any White cat, any White politician, can. Instead, we have Nixon, who, I don't know what he's going to do."

Then Davis added: "I'm sick of talking about what caused the racial situation in America. We know all about that. Now we should be talking about what we are going to do about it. Where do we go from here, as human beings?"

Jan. 16, 1969

Sammy Davis: Renaissance Man

Sammy Davis Jr.

Despite this age of specialty, Renaissance man is not dead – he is, at least in one incarnation, alive and well at the Club Tropicoro of El San Juan Hotel.

Appearing there these evenings is Sammy Davis Jr., who sings as well as he dances, dances as well as he clowns, clowns as well as he does impressions, and does impressions that seem to sound more like the performers he imitates than they do, themselves.

Mixing Black soul with Jewish schmaltz and Puerto Rican sabor, Davis had Wednesday's opening night audience – which included New York Mayor John V. Lindsay – up in arms, at the end of which were hands that applauded louder and stronger as his one and one-half hour appearance grooved on.

While he starts off pleasantly enough – joking a bit about his mink-caped, cigarette holder entrance, belting out a nice ballad, "As Long As She Needs Me," scat singing and giving out with Carmen Miranda chica-chica-boom-chic sounds to a drum accompaniment – still, for the first 30 minutes, or so, he does not completely capture the audience. If this is the first time you've seen Davis on a night club stage, you might even wonder, Good, yes, but what's so great?

But then, gradually, comes the crossing over of that thin line, on one side of which is smiling appreciation, on the other, far side, is tingling involvement. Davis reached it opening night with a deepfelt "I Gotta Be Me," held it on a swinging "You're Nobody Till Somebody Loves You" and multiplied it on a medley of Ray Charles soul stirrings, in which he worked like a demon, shaking the very vines hanging from the ceiling of the club, which he had early described as being decorated in "early jungle."

He admits at the beginning of the medley that he is no Ray Charles, and he's right; still, he was at his very best in this tribute to the genius of soul music. Davis is at his very best when, as he did here, he wraps himself completely into what he is doing, seeming to reach down inside himself, almost oblivious to the audience, brows furrowing body and voice exploding in – an amazing intensity of feeling and rhythm.

At those times, Sammy Davis becomes what so many people say he is: the best entertainer around today.

He closes with "What Kind of Fool Am I," demonstrating how Billy Eckstine, Vaughn Monroe, Mel Torme, Louis Armstrong, Dean Martin and, of course, Sammy Davis would do it.

Jan. 3, 1969

City Side

Budd Schulberg and Elia Kazan would like to shout it from Los Picachos (the highest mountain in Puerto Rico). The film they plan to begin shooting here next February will not—repeat NOT—in any way, shape, form or fancy resemble Oscar Lewis's *La Vida*. While screenwriter Schulberg and director Kazan had earlier considered a film based partially on Lewis's work, they have now decided that *La Vida* doesn't begin to touch on the life and hard times of the Puerto Rican people. Therefore, Schulberg has written an original screenplay from which the movie will be made.

The movie will contain one 45-second scene in La Perla, setting of the Lewis book, Schulberg said in an interview here Monday. But the scene is just "a walk through, a tour, a piece of geography," according to the author. "Last spring, when we visited here, we caught an awful lot of flak about *La Vida*," Schulberg said. "And we tried to tell people we weren't going to depend solely on the book, but we were in a difficult position because we had no script. Well, now we have a completed script and a lot of people in the Puerto Rican community, both here and in New York, have read it and the response has been heartening. We now feel that *La Vida* was a problem of spring, 1969, and we're now moving on to the problem of making the film in the best possible manner."

What the film will try to portray is one Puerto Rican family's physical and spiritual journey from the mountains, from which they are dispossessed, to the slums of San Juan, to the streets of New York. The movie will be called "In the Streets," because, as Pito, the young protagonist says, "That's where it's at." Meaning that's where, for him and his generation, the knowledge and the relevant action is, and that's where, according to Schulberg and Kazan, "the struggle is and the problem is going to be met." That, also, is where much of the film will be shot.

The movie will center on the problem of—here comes that word again—identity, as "any honest film about Puerto Rico would have to," said Schulberg, who sees this theme as a symbol of the reappraisal and change the whole world is going through.

"Individuals throughout the world are asking, 'Who am I?' People collectively are trying to decide: 'Who should we belong to?' That, for instance, is the anguish of the Blacks in the United States. And that is something that is especially focused here in Puerto Rico. This may sound too sociological, but we hope to tell in the film a story that entertains through the development of one individual and his family."

Schulberg and Kazan will apply to Fomento in the next few weeks for permission to set up a company here through which *In the Streets*, "and possibly other films," would be made. Schulberg said: "We think it's the first serious film about Puerto Rico—as far as we know—and the logical thing would be to base it here, both economically and culturally... If *In the Streets*; and other movies we may make here are successful, it could be a great shot in the arm for a local film industry. Our feeling is that too many opportunists have come here in the past, offering themselves as important filmmakers from the mainland, who have had neither substantial ideas for films nor the standing they claimed in the film industry."

For those who haven't been inside a moving picture house since the days of Clara Bow,

it should he pointed out that Kazan and Schulberg have, to say the least, the standing. Kazan has won two Academy Awards, for *Gentleman's Agreement* and *On the Waterfront*, and has also directed such films as *Viva Zapata, A Streetcar Named Desire* and *America, America.* Schulberg won an Oscar for the "Waterfront" screenplay and has also worked with Kazan on the highly acclaimed, if seldom seen, *A Face in the Crowd.*

Schulberg thinks that Puerto Rico, with its climate, physical surroundings and talent— "We're convinced there is a real pool of talent here"—could be a world center for film making. "We feel that no one has come here to really put it together. That's why, after being advised by several prominent local people, we feel that Fomento is our first logical step."

Schulberg and Kazan took a one-day trip Sunday to Culebra and found it "fascinating" in several aspects, including as a set for movies. "There are fantastic highlands there that look like Scotland and Ireland and there are beaches more beautiful than in St. John. "Maybe," Schulberg said, "the best thing would be for the Navy to withdraw and let us make films there."

Aug. 18, 1970

He's Got Some Offers
You Can't Refuse

Bernie, it seems, has a problem. At least, he's got questions and he's on the phone from the States talking it over with Sol Geltman. Sol Geltman has the answers, "What I want to leave you with Bernie, is this: if you muster the group, we'll offer a package that, like they say in *The Godfather*, you can't turn down."

So the quote isn't exact. But the sentiment is. Sol Geltman is offering packages at the Helio Isla (once San Jeronimo) Hotel that any self-respecting conspicuous consumer can't possibly refuse. Eight—count 'em, eight!—restaurants, a string of new bars, a recently air-conditioned lobby that protects the coiffed heads of the guests from those messy ocean breezes, a ballroom-turned-theater restaurant, a game room with pool, ping pong and air hockey tables and assorted pinball machines, new carpets, new furniture, new furnishings, new lights—all part of a $1.8 million refurbishing job. And to top it off, the whipped cream on the icing, is a lineup this coming season that sounds like guests for a

telethon, entertainment you—and Sol couldn't refuse.

After Aponte Caratini made the purchase, he turned the operating over to Helio Hotels Corp. The hotel got a new name: the Helio Isla. It also got a new president and managing director: Sol Geltman. And it's hoping to the tune of several million dollars (refurbishing, superstars, ads on the mainland) to get a brand new image.

Sol Geltman, in case you don't remember, is one of those wonderful people who gave you El San Juan Hotel. At least, he was managing director and vice president from 1963–66, at a time when El San Juan was in the throes of becoming what it is today: Paradise, as materialized from the dreams of the ten-inch-cigar, pinky-ring set. Geltman's training ground was Miami Beach, where he was food and beverage director for some of the Big Ones—Algiers, Eden Roc, Fontainebleau—between 1951 and 1962. After he left El San Juan, he made his pilgrimage to the hoteliers' Mecca: Las Vegas, where he stayed a year, admitting to haying helped build the former Bonanza, now M-G-M Grand Hotel. Another poster adorning another of Geltman's office walls tells all about the new owners and their modest resort: "*The Folks Who Conquered the Roman Empire, Lost the Civil War, Smashed the Third Reich, and Charted the Universe... Now Give You Las Vegas... A $100 Million Dollar Fantasy... 2,100 Rooms And Suites.*"

"Why think small," said Sol Geltman, "when you can think big."

***

You sit in Sol Geltman's incredibly people-and-paper crowded office and watch and listen to the passing parade. Here they come, there they go. They're in, they're out, they're back. Aging men in mod clothes. Guys with *two* pinky rings. Sixty-year-old women with ash blonde hair. Geltman, always cool, takes it all in stride, all the wheeling, dealing, complaints, compliments, offers that can't be refused. He throws off Don Rickles insults to friends, and others, all with a little boy's impish grin. Introducing the hotel's projects manager and the reporter to one another: "This is Sy Glick. Sy Glick is what makes Sammy

run. This is Bob Friedman. Bob works for the San Juan *Star.* You give the *Star* the facts and they'll distort them. But only 90 percent of the time."

Secretary steps into the office. "Mr. Geltman, I have a Mrs. "B" here. She says Seymour Herbs sends regards and that she bought a $50 ticket for the New Year's Eve show and they gave her a $40 seat." Sol Geltman's blue eyes gaze forward from behind his half-lensed reading glasses. "Seymour Herbs? Oh, yeah, give her a refund on the difference."

After a while, Mrs. "B" is unsatisfied with the partialness of the refund. She storms into the office. She smiles but her mouth is twitching around the edges. "We were treated like cattle," she says. "We only got served dinner after we slipped the waiter a $20 bill. My husband is in business here. He's a gentleman, so he paid his bill. He should have walked out without paying, like many of the others did. I've been here two days about this."

Sol Geltman sits back in his swivel chair. He looks at Mrs. "B" over his half glasses. He is deadpan. He doesn't bat one lash. "Tell your husband to write me a letter," he says in soft, cool tones. "I'll take care of it."

Mrs. "B" storms out of the office.

"*Everyone* wants a ringside table," says Sol Geltman.

***

"There are two great hotels here," according to Geltman. "El San Juan and the Caribe Hilton. We want to be the third. How are we going to do this? By creating the image of fine dining, entertainment and resort living. Today's tourist is not the same as the tourist of 10, even five, years ago. Today's tourist isn't just content with the sun, cocktails, dinner and a show. He wants the best. He wants *two* shows. He wants to stay at a hotel where the top stars are performing to boost his own status.

"If you give them top entertainment, they'll come back to enjoy it, even the youngsters will find someone to take them to see it. Where there's a will, there's a relative."

***

It's another day. Sol Geltman is not in what you would call a good mood. He's had overbooking problems in the morning, pesky reporter problems at lunch.

The reporter had heard earlier from a reliable source that Liza Minnelli was getting $75,000 a week for her Helio Isla appearance and he wondered if that was a record for the island. "About the $75,000 Liza Minnelli is getting..."

"Now you've turned me off," Geltman, who was dimming to the questions all morning, announced. "I don't discuss performers' salaries. Especially the way you brought it up. I know that ruse. Her salary isn't news.

"You newspaper guys are always looking for something to start trouble. You're always so negative. You want to write about something, write how Carmita Jimenez is going to be the opening act in the Jerry Lewis show. It's such a wonderful break for her. Write about how we are conditioned the lobby of the hotel so our guests could be comfortable. That's news."

And while he was at it, why is the newspaper so much against tourism? The newspaper isn't against tourism, the reporter said, but it did question the value of some of the aspects and...

"What are you talking about? Do you know what you're talking about? You don't know what you're talking about. Tourism is the second largest industry on the island, (actually it's third, after manufacturing and construction) $250 million a year. You keep being against that and kill the industry and you'll see what happens to Puerto Rico.

"And now you got a campaign against slot machines." He gave a head-shaking sign to show his disdain at the provincialism of it all. "Why don't you have a campaign against drugs or against rum? What about all the drunken drivers' that rum causes? How about a campaign against them?"

Then Geltman cooled off and gave his little boy, impish smile. The reporter waited for the zinger. But Geltman came up with a surprisingly philosophical one-liner. "I never heard of a slot machine," he said, "that killed a person."

Jan. 9, 1974

Sol Geltman and the entertainers booked into the Helio Isla Hotel, from top: Sammy Davis Jr., Liza Minelli, Jerry Lewis, Tom Jones, Paul Anka, and Alan King. (*Star* photo by José García)

114

Dizzy Gillespie and the Roots of Jazz

Dizzy Gillespie, 55, goatee turned gray, belly puffed like his cheeks when he blows his trumpet, winced. He had been asked: "What made you and Charlie Parker and the other founders of 'bop' music break with the past?"

"It wasn't a break. It was evolution. A little bit at a time. The musician who comes later is no greater than the one who came before. If you break with the past," said Dizzy, "it's your ass."

***

Thursday night at the Flamboyan Hotel. The Gillespie Quartet plays a special midnight show for local musicians. They almost blow the hotel into the lagoon with their opening number. "Sunshine." Dizzy runs nervously up and down the scales, then sends off long, loud, clarion blasts, while the rhythm section—drummer Mickey Roker, guitarist Al Gafa and bassist Earl May—pulse madly behind him. Vocalist Dede Bridgewater stills the house with an amazingly graceful, supple "Here Comes That Rainy Day," then brings it down with an incredible blues. Dizzy asks local musicians to join him for his last number. "You know," he says, his torso bending back from the waist, his head lolling from side to side, "I was the first North American musician to use Latin Sounds." The audience of musicians cheer. They know "Manteca" and "Night in Tunesia" and the part Gillespie played in welding Afro-Cuban and American jazz sounds. Sabucito—nephew of the great Latin percussionist Sabu—jumps onto the stage, rips off his jacket and, for the next fifteen minutes, brings forth from the conga drums sounds as old and as new as the first and the last man.

***

Gillespie said he first became interested in Latin music in 1937 at the Savoy Ballroom in Harlem. "I was working there with the Teddy Hill and Edgar Hayes bands. The relief band was led by Alberto Socarras, a Cuban flute player and a bad mother. The music fascinated me. We had the same mother from Africa, but Cubans were closer to Africa than we American Blacks were. In Cuba, they didn't take the drums away from the slaves like they did in America. They took the drums away from us because they were afraid of rebellion. You could talk with drums."

In 1947, Gillespie, who had also played often with musicians from the Cuban orchestra of Machito, added Cuban drummer Chano Pozo to his band.

"When you write down Chano Pozo," said Gillespie, "put down 'messiah'. He was on the same level as Charlie Parker in his contribution to jazz."

'Bop' music came to flower in the early 1940's at musicians' hangouts in Harlem, particularly Minton's Playhouse. The new style was the most radical change in jazz history, giving rise to the whole category of what is now considered modern Jazz. Gillespie and alto saxist Charlie Parker are generally considered the two most important figures in the bop movement. Parker was a brilliant musician with a tortured soul who died at the age of 35. Gillespie never seemed to take himself half as seriously as did music critics and jazz fans all over the world. In

the early days of 'bop,' he set a new fashion among his followers, who copied his goatee, beret and horn-rimmed glasses. He always clowned on stage. But behind the mask, most agreed, was one of the giants of jazz, second only to Louis Armstrong in the innovations he brought to the trumpet.

***

Dizzy Gillespie addresses several hundred students Friday afternoon at Sacred Heart College in Santurce. He gives a short personal, ironically humorous history of jazz. He notes in the talk that one thing blacks and Puerto Ricans have in common is that "we both get the sh—y end of the stick." The audience cheers. A very pretty, dark-eyed female student rises to ask a question. Gillespie invites her on stage. She wants to know how the political, religious and sociological tendencies he expounded in his talk find their way into his music. He ogles her in soft, comic appreciation, then says:

"I belong to the Baha'i faith which teaches us we're all on the same source, but all supposed to retain our ethnic differences. You've got to retain your own heritage, but only with the idea of making the whole more beautiful. What you bring has got to jive with unity.

"And that's the same with my music. In my group, all the instruments are different. And like it should be with the different races in the world, I tell the musicians to hold on to their particular thing and jive together."

***

"In the beginning," said Dizzy Gillespie, "there was Buddy Bolden, one of the original creators of the trumpet (circa 1890, New Orleans). At that time, that were maybe 15 trumpet players in the United States.

"Then Bolden got a protégé, King Oliver who learned from him. King Oliver then told himself, 'What I learned I can take and then do this.' Through evolution, he had a new style on the trumpet.

"Then came Louis. He learned all he could from King Oliver, added new riffs and had a new style. By that time, maybe there were tens of thousands of trumpet players.

"Next, Roy Eldridge came on the scene. He took from Louis, from Red Allen, from Rex Stewart and added his own. At that time, I was down in South Carolina and I use to hear Roy Eldridge on the radio once a week from the Savoy ballroom and I told myself, 'Oh, that is it!'

"I met Charlie Shavers in Philadelphia who knew all Roy's solos and I copied them and kept playing like that til 1938. But I was looking for more. I got inspiration from chords on the piano, from (pianist) Art Tatum and from (saxophonists) Coleman Hawkins and Benny Carter. From all that, I created a new style. And by that time the hundreds of thousands of trumpet players are copying my style all over the world.

"After, there's Miles (Davis) and Fats Navarro. They both went different ways. Clifford Brown and Lee Morgan and Freddie Hubbard come from Fats, Nat Adderly and others from the Miles school.

"And on and on and on," said Dizzy Gillespie with a hand motion that suggested an infinity of trumpet players, each evolving from the other, each tapping roots to discover a new branch, blowing weird yet strangely familiar sounds into the lives of our children's children's children's children's."

Oct. 21, 1973

Dizzy Gillespie (*Star* Photo by Rafael H. Trias)

Cary Grant Says He's 'Over the Hill'

The time has come. No one thought it would ever come. And who could be presumptuous enough to think it ever could come?

But Cary Grant says the time has come. "I'm kind of going over the hill. I think my romantic lead days are over. I'm getting kind of past that now. Wouldn't you say so?"

Unfortunately, no opinion could be given as to how far decrepitation has set in, for the interview with the 63-year-old film star was taking place over the telephone, the evening before Grant was to depart after a brief vacation at the Americana Hotel here. However, usually reliable sources reported that the man who has been the romantic screen lead to almost all of the movie Women that mattered – from Mae West to Grace Kelly, with Marlene Dietrich and Ingrid Bergman somewhere in between – looks, as of earlier this week when he was spotted in Old San Juan, as he has been looking for what seems like the past several decades – suntanned, handsome,

suave; looking, in fact, just like... Cary Grant!

Yet he was talking of "searching for other (than romantic) roles" or maybe even quitting the screen for good.

"I retired ten years ago, you know, and went on a trip around the world. But I got tired of that, so I started to work again. Now, I just may retire again. Or I may go on searching for other roles. I really never know what I will do tomorrow."

There have been articles published which said that one way Grant looks like a young 40 at age 60 is through the practice of yoga. But the self-proclaimed senior citizen said the other day that all reports of his yogism have been greatly exaggerated.

"I don't know a damn thing about it," he declared. "That was just a story that got around. I don't practice yoga, but I admire the people who do. We are all searching for something. Anything is better than what society has to offer."

The conversation turned to present-day society's most publicized critics – the hippies.

"Some think of the hippies as only rebels," Grant said. "But I don't. The Christians were also looked on as rebels. But their rebellion succeeded and they persisted and came through with a philosophy of love. They were the hippies of their day. That's my point of view."

"I hope the hippies find what they are looking for. And if they do, I hope they tell me."

And – back to the films – are movies better today than they were in the 1930's and 1940's?

"Yes they're definitely better. The good ones, that is. The older films couldn't compete with the outstanding films of today – especially on a technical level."

But Grant doesn't think that the Hollywood of thirty years ago was as divorced from reality as many now feel it was. It's just the subject matter was different.

"In those days, you had a lot of films that gently poked fun at the rich. And though the separation then between the filmgoer and the subject of the films was greater than today, the rich did exist. And in films like, The Philadelphia Story and Dinner at Eight you knew these people. A picture about Buckingham Palace can be just as realistic as a picture about a garbage can, if it is researched.

His favorite film? *The Philadelphia Story? Indiscreet? Blonde Venus? Gunga Din? North by Northwest? Suspicion? To Catch a Thief? Notorious? Night and Day? None But the Lonely Heart? The Talk of the Town? Arsenic and Old Lace? Penny Serenade? My Favorite Wife? Only Angels Have Wings? Holiday? The Awful Truth? Topper? She Done Him Wrong?*

"In a strange way, they're all my favorites. I select my pictures. I do what I want to do."

Well, then which film did he consider his biggest flop?

"I suppose it was *The Pride and the Passion.* I think I look silly in a costume. The public thought so too. They wouldn't accept me, or Sinatra (who was also in the film) looking that way. Still, we had a marvelous time making the film, spending four months in Spain. That also is important. Enjoying wha you are doing. And doing what you want to do."

But doesn't he still enjoy making films and still want to make them?

"Yes, but one knows when one's time is waning. While we are living, we are dying."

Then, bucking up – one could almost see the hand go up to the knot of the tie, the head cock back jauntily – he added:

"On the other hand, while we are dying we should also be living."

January 6, 1968

Cary Grant

The Sporting Scene

*T*he sports scene during the years I lived on the island was brightly lit with terrific Puerto Rican athletes, home-grown and New York-raised. While I was too late to see the Santurce Crabbers of 1954, when Roberto Clemente and Willy Mays played side-by-side in the same outfield, the rosters of the baseball teams in the Puerto Rico Winter League were filled with future and current Major Leaguers, many island-born, like future Hall of Famers Orlando "Peruchín" Cepeda and Roberto Alomar, not to mention such big league all-stars as Juan "Igor" González, Bernie Williams, Carlos Baerga. Other Winter Leaguers included Baseball Hall of Famers Reggie Jackson, Mike Schmidt and Johnny Bench. If you were lucky, you could get a seat in Hiram Bithorn Stadium near former New York Giants pitcher Rubén Gómez, the first Puerto Rican to ever pitch in a World Series (1954), who was at all the Santurce Crabbers games and had many humorous and trenchant things to say as the game progressed.

Basketball started coming into its own on the island in the 1970s-80s. Many of the teams around the island were loaded with Puerto Ricans who learned their basketball smarts in and around New York (See story below). During those years, local hoop stars included notable players like Butch Lee, who was the first Puerto Rican and Latin American player to enter the National Basketball Association when he was drafted in 1978 by the Atlantic Hawks. Decades later, it was revealed that the Brooklyn-born-and-raised Carmelo "Melo" Anthony, one of the all-time great scorers of the NBA, had Puerto Rican roots. The one-time New York Knick was born in Brooklyn of an African-American mother and a Puerto Rican father.

The 1979 Pan American Games in Puerto Rico was when and where Bobby Knight, the U.S. team's basketball coach, went haywire. He was charged with punching a cop, and saying lovely things about the island, calling it "a hell hole," and worse, and, as reported in *The New York Times,* the coach pulled down his pants to "moon" the island as his flight took off back to the states.

Knight's nutty behavior began when the U.S. team was finishing a practice at Espiritu Santo High School outside San Juan and the Brazilian women's team entered the gym. They supposedly arrived early and Knight complained to policeman José D. Silva, who was guarding the gym entrance. Silva supposedly told Knight to cool it. Silva and Knight then reportedly got into a heated argument. Each claimed the other struck the first blow. Silva put Knight under arrest, handcuffed him and took him to a police station. Although the police later dropped the matter, Silva filed assault charges in San Juan District Court. Knight counter-filed. Knight was ordered to stand trial and his counter- charges were dismissed.

The U.S. won the basketball championship, defeating a scrappy island team 113-94 in the finals. Among other players, the U.S, team had such future all-time pro basketball greats on the court at Roberto Clemente Coliseum as Isaiah Thomas and 7-ft., 4-in. Ralph Sampson. When the U.S. players lined up to receive their gold medals, Knight stood in a comer of the court, getting continually booed. With several reporters around him, Knight said of the island population, in general:

"f--- 'em, .f--- 'em all. I'll tell you what. Their basketball is a hell of a lot easier to beat than their court system. The only f-----g thing they know how to do is grow bananas."

Since Knight cut out before the trial against him was held, the Commonwealth government put out a warrant for his arrest, but he was not extradited. Puerto Rico canceled the warrant in the late 1980 after Knight apologized to Puerto Ricans for the incident.

A sidebar: Many of the U.S. journalists covering the games couldn't understand why so many Puerto Ricans were rooting against the U.S. team during several contests, cheering on even the Cubans. Most of the journalists couldn't quite accept the latent Latinism shown by the fans. During those years, Puerto Rican boxing champs, like Carlos Ortiz, Wilfred Benítez, Wilfredo Gómez and José "Chegui" Torres brought excitement to the island, whether in bouts held in Puerto Rico or, more likely, as seen over television from such boxing capitals of the time as New York and Las Vegas. I remember watching Carlos Ortiz defend his championship in 1965. I had a ringside seat on a wooden box in front of the public TV set in Plaza de Armas in Old San Juan.

Muhammed Ali, the heavyweight champion of the world, fought twice in Puerto Rico. The first time, still called

Cassius Clay, he came to the island in 1965 for a three- round exhibition fight where he battered around his opponent. Clay's exhibition was the preliminary for a bout between José Torres, then the world light-heavyweight champ, and Tom McNeeley. Torres won easily in a 10-round decision. The fights were at Hiram Bithorn Stadium in Hato Rey.

While several American writers, including Ernest Hemingway and Noman Mailer, made pretenses of wanting a career in the ring, the Playa de Ponce-born Torres may have been the only boxing champ who wanted to be a writer. He gave boxing lessons to Mailer in exchange for literary critique of his writing efforts, and went on after his retirement to write columns for the *New York Post* and a book about Ali (Sting like a Bee.)

Included is an interview I did with Ali while he was on the island preparing for a second fight, this one in 1976 at Roberto Clemente Coliseum to defend his world championship against Jean-Pierre Coopman of Belgium.

5 kids off sidewalks of New York vs. U.S.

San Juan (Special)—It's New York versus the U.S. for the Pan Am games basketball gold medal.

Well, just about.

Bobby Knight's U.S. squad clashes tonight, in a game that will decide the basketball championship, with a team representing Puerto Rico. Eight members of that Puerto Rican squad, including the starting five, got their basketball smarts in the parks and projects of New York, where they grew up.

"Just about all of us learned the game crashing boards and playing street ball in New York," said team captain and starting center Charlie Bermudez "When you're learning basketball in the streets of New York you're learning with the best."

Bermudez, who began learning the game as a teenager in the Jacob Riis projects on the lower East Side, was all-city in 1968 when he played for Adelphi Academy in Brooklyn. He is one of three former New York High School All Stars on the Puerto Rican team. Ray Dalmau, at 30 the oldest team member, was All-Metro in 1966 when he led Benjamin Franklin High School in the Bronx in scoring, and Nestor Cora made All-City in 1974 while playing for Adlai Stevenson also in the Bronx. Cora went on to play his freshman year at Fordham, where he was picked for the All-Tournament team during the 1974–75 Holiday Festival, and was a starter for the past two years at St. Francis.

Forward Rubén Rodríguez broke scoring and rebounding records at Long Island University and Georgie Torres, the fifth starter, picked up the basic moves in the South Bronx's Patterson Projects, which gave the basketball world Nate "Tiny" Archibald and Ricky Sobers, among many others.

Cesar Fantauzzi, born and bred in Harlem's El Barrio, played his high school ball at Ignatius Rice; Angelo Cruz was on the DeWitt Clinton team in the Bronx, and Willie Quinones plays for Mercer Junior College in New Jersey.

The Puerto Rican squad was chosen from the Island-wide amateur Superior League, where each team plays a 36-game season and as many as 20 playoff games. In the past few years, basketball has replaced baseball as the No. 1 sport here and interest for tonight's (Friday) U.S.-Puerto Rico game is at fever pitch. Any mixed emotions the New York-raised members of the Puerto Rican team may have in trying to cut down to size their stateside brothers has been submerged in a heady rush of Puerto Rican nationalism during the games, in general, and for tonight's shootout in particular.

"For this game, I feel very Puerto Rican," said New York-born Rubén Rodriguez.

Both squads have sailed through the qualifying rounds and the finals undefeated. The U.S. has rolled past nine opponents and Puerto Rico has beaten eight up until last night, when they were schedule to take on Argentina.

Whether this comparatively small—the tallest man is 6'7"—but very scrappy bunch of New York Puerto Ricans can outplay the rest of the country will be decided starting 9 p.m., before a capacity crowd of 13,000 at Roberto Clemente Coliseum.

Jan. 9, 1979

Puerto Rico basketball team captain Charlie Bermúdez scores a basket against the U.S. team in the 1979 Pan Am Games in San Juan.

Going The Distance with Muhammed Ali

The short, broad-shouldered guy with arms like a weight-lifter and belly like a beer drinker was very insistent. He wore a white tee shirt with the words "Puerto Rico, Jackpot" and a picture of an overflowing slot machine stamped on it.

"I am all the way down from Montreal," he told the fellow from Salsa Productions, "and I want a picture with him."

"Sorry," the fellow said, "I can't arrange it."

"Look, it cost me $170 to come down here one way," the guy said. "I have to have a picture with him."

"We've got 200 people coming in from Belgium," said the fellow, "and it's going to cost them a lot more than $170.

"Of course," the guy said. "He's the God."

Funny, Jacques Dessurault doesn't look like your ordinary "groupie." But he says he's been following Muhammad Ali wherever the heavyweight champ has been fighting since his 1966 bout with Cleveland Williams in Houston. "I've been at both Frazier fights. And I was at the Foreman fight in India."

He means, of course, Africa, right?

Jacques, a pipe coverer for Union Carbide in Montreal, shrugs: India, Africa, what's the difference? He didn't go there for the sightseeing, He went—at a cost of $895—to see Ali wreck Foreman. And now he's spending a vacation with his wife in Puerto Rico to watch the champ crush his next opponent, Jean Pierre Coopman of Belgium.

"I want a picture with him to show my friends," said Dessurault, "so they'll believe I was here."

***

Susi has only been following Ali since three years ago, when she met him in Beirut. She missed out on his Manila fight with Frazier, but she saw him again when he recently boxed an exhibition in the Bahamas.

Susi says she's 22, looks 16. She's from Houston, she says, and "in the oil business." Someone who has been observing her the last few days says she spends money like if she's not in oil, she's got a rich relative who is. "She gives out ten-dollar tips like they were dimes." Said the observer, "and she keeps buying new cameras to take pictures of Ali during his workouts."

"God brought us together," said Susi. "He (God) spoke to me in Beirut and said I was to follow him (Ali)."

So, what else was new Tuesday at El San Juan Hotel where Muhammad Ali is preparing for his heavyweight championship fight against Jean Pierre Coopman Feb, 20 at Clemente Coliseum?

Well, you could buy in the hotel's upper lobby an "I Like Ali" tee shirt for $3, a "Float Like a Butterfly, Sting Like a Bee" pin for $1, a copy of "My Own Story" by Ali and Richard Durham for $11, an eight-by-ten glossy photo of the champ for $1. And for $5, you could attend his hour-long training session in the hotel's grand ballroom. (Drinks were available at a bar in the ballroom at $2 each—scotch, rum or whatever.)

Arnold Benus of Salsa Productions, which is co-promoting the Ali-Coopman fight with Don King, wanted it known that his group, not the hotel, has put the $5 entrance fee on the training sessions. "We have the rights for everything in Puerto Rico," Benus said.

He said calls are coming in from "all over" for fight tickets. "We already have more than 3,000 reservations," he said, "including at least one plane load of people coming from Belgium."

Benus said several hundred people have been attending the daily workouts. "When Ali gets going," he said, "it's the best show in town."

And then, the big moment, Ali walks down the lobby in white terrycloth robe. A woman walks up to him, touches his arm, says, "Oh, you're so beautiful!" Her voice cracks on the last word. Ali smiles, like he hasn't been telling the world the same thing for the last 12 years.

No one pays any attention to the sign at the entrance saying positively no pictures while Ali is training. Flashbulbs pop all over the ballroom while Ali is oiled down, his hands are bandaged, he works out on the big bag. Jacques, from Montreal, looks concerned. "He's too fat," he says. But then he brightens. "He'll lose weight in time for the fight. It's going to be all right" he says.

Suzi, from Houston, sits in the front row, her eyes glued to the champ.

Ali spars two uneventful rounds with Jimmy Ellis, then three more with Bobick, the last of which brings cheers from the crowd as he batters Bobick around the ring. Then, silent for the whole hour, he leans over the ropes and addresses the spectators.

"What you've just seen," he tells the audience, "is a nice light workout. There's a man in Belgium right now who's being fed raw meat to get ready to fight me. He's being told, 'you can whip him, you can whip him, you can put Belgium on the map'."

Ali shakes his head. He knows his gain will be the Atlas's loss. "I know I'm the greatest fighter of all time," he says. "I can whip any man in the whole world. Do you realize that's one hell of a statement to make?"

"He's not too sharp today," says a veteran Ali watcher. "I saw this routine a few days ago. He's best when he gets a heckler."

Unfortunately, Ali meets only with reverence from Tuesday's audience.

Following the workout, Ali is interviewed in his suite of rooms. With the unselfconsciousness of the professional athlete, he takes off his boxing trunks and puts on another robe and is naked for a few seconds. He's all supple muscle, from wide neck to powerful shanks, and looks like the classical statues of athletes from ancient Greece.

He leans back on his bed, ready for the interview. Ali might very well hold the all-time newspaper copy record, so what can you ask him that he hasn't spouted off, joked or philosophized about a thousand times before? Well, the reporter starts off absurdly by asking Ali if he's happy.

Ali pauses for several seconds, as though contemplating all the ramifications of the question. Then he says: "Very few can say they are happy. Almost everyone will say he or she is unhappy one way or the other. Some are unhappy because they can't reach the power they have strived for. Others because they have not gained the worldly possessions they sought. Still others because the love they have for someone is not returned..."

Ali continues: "Deep within man there is a yearning. He who is really happy, he who is truly happy, will be happy everywhere and anywhere, in a palace or in a shack, in rags or in riches."

Reporter starts on another subject. Ali tells him to hold on, he's not finished yet.

"The happy man," he says, "has discovered the fountain of true happiness, which is the knowledge of the purpose of life. I know my purpose. I wanted to be the first and most famous Black man in America to be free of white forces. The first Black man to do and say whatever he wants, so that people can say, 'there's one that didn't Uncle Tom.' I have the most recognized face on the planet. My purpose is to use this for God and my mission to spread the word of my (Muslim) religion."

Someone brings Ali his biography to autograph. Ali writes then reads aloud: "Death is so near and time for friendly actions so limited."

Ali looks significantly at the reporter. Reporter looks at Ali, nods.

"That's an original quote," says Ali. Then he says: "I want you to hear some of this," he clucks his tongue twice "that's the way I call my people," he says. A tall lovely young woman materializes from another room.

"Bring me my speech," Ali says.

She returns with a two-inch-thick stack of large index cards.

"I'm working on this lecture I'm going to be giving somewheres in New York to 1,500 women who are studying to be pediatricians. I'll give you a couple of lines."

"The soul of an infant is like a photographic plate which has never been exposed before..."

About 15 speech minutes later, a waiter comes into the suite with a meal for someone. Whoever ordered it is not in the immediate vicinity, but Ali signs for it. He adds a tip. "That's a five-dollar tip," he tells the waiter.

"Thank you," says the waiter politely, but with dignified reserve.

Back to the interview. How does he feel now about being stripped of the heavyweight crown back in 1968 for refusing to serve in the Army during the Vietnam War?

"That's the best thing that ever happened to me. It showed that I was a strong man. I stuck to my ideals and made more converts for my religion," Ali said.

Does he ever have fears of advancing age, of losing his speed and stamina, of being less than the great athlete he is?

"Life is a continual liar, a great deceiver and a tricky evil-doer. It's glories and fame and successes are short lived. They fade and they decay with speedy exhaustion..." Time passes. The reporter listens, pretends to listen, takes notes, pretends to take notes. He's feeling as groggy from the flurry of words as one of Ali's ring opponents must feel from the champ's merciless jabs.

"Pyramids crumbling... Something everlasting... Spirit... Resurrection... Rivers lakes streams... Different names... Contain the same water... I have a lecture called the inner life. That's I-N-N-E-R... Where is man's wealth... Wealth is in his knowledge..."

A pause. An Ali cluck of the tongue. Young woman brings in ice water. Reporter hears himself asking questions about politics.

"Politics is built on change and destruction... Kissinger wants to talk to me..."

Ali goes on but then something he says makes the reporter shoot up in his chair. Would he repeat that last statement?

"I said," Ali repeats, "the limelight is not what keeps me going. The day I can drop out of the limelight, I'll be happy."

The reporter thinks he would bet on Coopman for a one round KO of Ali than on that.

Jan. 29, 1976

**Jacques Dessurault of Montreal meets
Muhammad Ali. (*Star* Photo by David Acevedo)**

Idioma Impositions

*T*he Andalusians brought their form of Spanish when they settled on the island in the 15th and 16th Centuries. They picked up some words from the Taínos, such as *hamaca*, *huracán* and *tabaco*. Slaves brought from Africa put in a word or two, such as *gandul* (pigeon pea) and *malanga* (root vegetable). Then, after the U.S. took over the island, came the Official Language Act of 1902, making both English and Spanish the *idiomas del país*. That law also made English the obligatory language of instruction in island public schools, whether the natives liked it or not. The highly ambivalent practice ended in 1948.

While, according to Census figures, only about one out of every five island inhabitants were bilingual in the 1980s, the battle over the role of Spanish and English in Puerto Rico was, more or less, continual. Partisan politics and language policy often were tied to one another. In 1991, the Commonwealth-backing Popular Democratic Party established Spanish as the one and only official language of the island. In 1993 the statehood-supporting New Progressive Party revoked the Spanish Only law to, once more, bring English and Spanish together for island officialdom. The political maneuverings played it sort-of safe. The pro-Commonwealth law did not change the policy of promoting both languages in the schools; the stake-holders insisted that no way would Spanish be eliminated on the island when Puerto Rico became the 51st state.

Independentistas, and others, saw Puerto Rico as a Spanish-speaking country, and efforts to impose English on the populace as a way to try again to Americanize the island while minimizing its culture.

Here is what master Spanish-to-English translator Gregory Rabassa had to say about writers and translators working in Spanish and English and both.

On writing, Spanish, and the 'language of the Raj'

You may find this one hard to believe, but Nobel Prize-winner Gabriel García Márquez, actually prefers the English language translation of his "One Hundred Years of Solitude," already a classic of Latin American literature, to the Spanish original.

Who says so? Gregory Rabassa, the translator, that's who. "I think García Márquez was referring to the 'sound'," said the man who helped ignite the "boom" that sent Latin American writers blasting off into worldwide literary recognition. Rabassa has translated, among others, García Márquez, Mario Vargas Llosa of Peru, Jorge Amado of Brazil, Julio Cortázar of Argentina and Puerto Rico's Luis Rafael "La Guaracha del Macho Camacho" Sánchez.

Was the great Colombian writer talking tongue in Latin American cheek? Not necessarily, said Rabassa, who was in San Juan last week. "We were talking about the English language and García Márquez was saying that it was more expressive than Spanish. He said English had more sounds.

Even when compared with the other romance languages, Spanish doesn't have the open and closed vowels you get in Portuguese or French or Italian."

What Spanish does have is a logical organization that should have happened to the French, since they are so enamored with the principles of reasoning, not always found in their language. If you compare the languages, as Queens College (N.Y.) comparative literature professor Rabassa was asked to do, you find that "English, like Latin, has developed out of primitive roots, while Spanish and all the romance languages are a dialect of a very well-developed language."

Is that good or bad for Spanish-language writers? Neither, said master translator Rabassa, whose father was Cuban, but who only began classroom study of Spanish in college. "It only means that Spaniards have a different tool to work with."

Actually, the tight organization that "limits" the Spanish language might make for better writing, Rabassa said. In order to break out, Spanish writers have to be more adventurous than their English-language counterparts, who are always adventuring because the language lends itself to it.

Metaphors abound in Spanish just because it doesn't have the variety of other languages, said the translator.

The talk got around to the recent PEN International Congress in New York. Rabassa, an executive board member of the worldwide writers' organization, did not think the meeting was as anti-American as the press made it out to be, but acknowledged that the sentiment did exist among writers at the meeting. He feels, however, that Latin American writers have a "more complex attitude" toward the United States than their European counterparts and, consequently, Americans have more to learn from Latin American writers than from the Europeans.

"European writers tend to be a little simplistic about the United States," Rabassa said. "Latin American writers see more of the gray areas. European writers are more anti-American on the cultural level, but a lot of Latin American writers have lived in the states, and they seem to have more of a sympathetic feel for the day-to-day culture.

"Latin American writers are more opposed to the political and economic policies of the United States, which are tied in more with their own political experiences and their own lives. If Latin American writers are anti-American, they have better reasons for it."

Rabassa quoted Cuban patriot José Martí, who said of his experiences in the United States: "I have lived in the monster and I know its guts."

Martí discovered for Hispanics great American writers like Walt Whitman, but he also brought the news to Latin America of pending U.S. imperialism in the hemisphere, Rabassa noted.

Closer to home, things are different for Puerto Rican writers than for other Latin Americans. "The United States is actually here," Rabassa said. "It is an occupation, although a semi-benign one."

He added: "I hadn't noticed it when I was in Puerto Rico before, but this time I saw the U.S. flag flying over an old Spanish fort and I thought, 'My God, it's the Raj!'" He was, of course, referring to those days of the veddy British Empire in India.

In fact, Rabassa sees much of this recent *revolu* over the proposal to delay the teaching of English in public schools here linked to the perception of English as "the language of the Raj," i.e., the colonizer, i.e., the United States. "All the linguists I know say the earlier you teach a language, the better," he said. "I'll bet there wouldn't be so much of a dispute if the language in question was French, the language of culture, or German, a real foreign language."

The Puerto Rican writer who "handles the American presence best" is Luis Rafael Sánchez, according to the translator. "He sees the presence as just another circumstance. Maybe that is why he is the Puerto Rican writer understood best in Latin America."

On the other hand, a writer such as Pedro Juan Soto in his writings is "truly half in New York and half on the island," both places "quite legitimate" for him, leading to "good realistic" writing on his part, Rabassa said.

Writers being caught in their works between two worlds is something uniquely Puerto Rican nowadays in this hemisphere, Rabassa said.

"You don't have Italo-Americans writing about Italy, or Mexicans in Mexico writing about Mexicans living in Los Angeles, as you have Puerto Ricans writing about Puerto Ricans in New York," Rabassa said.

Semi-benign occupations, you could say, give writers the opportunity to hit home in more ways than one.

Feb. 3, 1986

137

Ex-Pats About Town

*T*hey came, they saw and they were conquered by Puerto Rico. And they left marks—good and bad--on the island during their stays. They were the many *extranjeros* who came to live on the island in the 1960s-1980s from such locales as far-away Poland and far-out East New York, Brooklyn.

D.I. Wolf, who lived many years on the island and ran a jewelry-souvenir shop in Old San Juan, escaped from his native Poland just before the Nazis took over the country. He usually met daily at La Bombonera restaurant with two other Jewish refugees who were jewelers and who had concentration camp numbers tattooed on their arms. Wolf, who had escaped to South Africa, considered himself "lucky beyond words."

Brooklyn-born-and-bred Tony Tursi was rumored to be the Mafia's main man in San Juan, which he always denied. He ran, among other seedy joints, La Riviera Club, located on the Puerta de Tierra waterfront. The club catered to the hookers-about-town, visiting seamen and tourists, expatri-ates and locals. His unsavory reputation did not keep him from running for mayor of San Juan in an ad-hoc campaign (see story below.) He spent several years in federal prison (also see story) and on his release in 1979, he "retired" to Las Vegas, where he died in 1989.

The Comeback of D.I. Wolf

"Listen, begin your story this way: 'When we last visited D.I. Wolf, we found him in tears and rags'—you can say that, tears and rags be dramatic!—'but now it's really good to come back and see the phoenix in the form of a human being rising from the ashes.' Begin it that way and the rest is up to you."

Alright: when we last visited D.I. Wolf things were looking down. The time was last August, about two weeks before the scheduled opening of his new art gallery on Plaza Colón. On the floor around him were scattered scores of mutilated paintings, including some of his own works and others by Puerto Rican painter Epifanio Irizarry. A job done by vandals. And maybe revenge-seeking others.

D.I. Wolf—born 68 years ago in Poland and living the past 20 years in Puerto Rico, where he has been trying for at least half that time to get backing for his Caribbean wonderland trade fair-amusement park project, was close to tears, if not in rags.

"When I walked in this morning," he said then, continually sweeping a hand over the knife-slashed paintings that were scattered about the floor, as though he hoped to sweep them back into shape and onto the walls, "there was a bottle of ammonia on the floor and I was ready to drink it. I lost just about everything."

Instead, he bought himself a bottle of champagne, drank to the part that died inside himself when he discovered the destruction; then, gradually, he restored and repaired and some ten months later, opened for business, pleasure, and assorted other needs.

"You can say that a lot of pain and effort went into fixing things up because I was working very hard and mourning at the same time. It cost a lot of money, but it was done with blood too. You can say, 'he showed his hands and there were cuts all over them'."

To try to sustain himself while the Borinquen Gallery gets off the ground, Wolf has opened a jewelry shop on the ground floor leading up to the first-floor gallery. "Put it this way: 'Mr Wolf has made himself a nice, neat jewelry shop; he's not afraid to have costume jewelry, which he advertises as fabulous fakes. He is apologetic about the store, but one cannot live by art alone'."

An assistant downstairs rings up a sale, Wolf says, "Hallelujah."

The 25 paintings and collages hanging on the gallery walls are all by Wolf. The 20 paintings by Irizarry that were mutilated will be restored by the artist when he comes to San Juan shortly from his Ponce home, Wolf said. He hopes soon to have exhibitions in his gallery of the works of other local artists.

While the interview is going on, a tourist couple comes into the gallery somewhat diffidently, unsure of entering into the world of the arts. The man is tall, early middle-age, with a soft round face, horn-rimmed glasses. He is dressed in sports clothes, but looks like he would be more comfortable in tie and jacket back in his Wichita, Kansas insurance office. His wife is blonde, attractive, more at ease than her husband. They look around at the colorful semi-abstract and abstract works that cover the walls.

As if to confirm the man's worst fears, Wolf, the artist, walks up to him while he is trying to make head-or-tail of a painting and asks: "What do you see?"

The man squints at the paneled-like abstraction, raises his eyebrows, makes a little jerk of his head to the side, smiles.

"I'll give you a hint," says Wolf. "There's four different scenes there. What comes in four parts? You should know. A little 12-year-old child told me."

The man smiles, reddens, shrugs.

"Maybe your wife would know. Women are more intelligent about these things."

The wife is also stumped. She smiles pleasantly as Wolf tries to coax the "four parts" from her. Finally, he says, "O.K., I'll tell you. It's the four seasons."

The couple nods. The wife says, "It's... unusual."

Wolf shows them another painting. They play the guessing game for a while until he tell them the colors splashing and sprouting across the canvas represented fireworks. "If you're American, that painting is the Fourth of July," he says. "If you're French, it's the Fourteenth of July. And it's the tenth of May if you're Polish.

The woman says: "It's very... fireworky."

Next, he explains to them his paean to the 'interdependence of man and machinery'. The work incorporates small metal wheels and cogs and painted factory scenes amidst swirls of color.

"I'm a working man," he says showing the couple his small rough scarred hands. "I don't hate machines. It's not the machine's fault if men let them run their lives."

The couple nods, as though Wolf had said what was on the tip of their tongues.

Wolf tells them about the Belgian poet Émile Verhaeren, who wrote poems in praise of the locomotive. "He was fascinated by their sound. One day, he was down on the tracks looking and listening real close to one and another came by and killed him."

The couple look at each other for a hint of the proper reaction. They settle for nods of condolence to Wolf, as though he were next of kin.

Next comes "Psychedelic Dream," an abstract blast of bright colors. He asks the man and his wife: "Have you ever taken drugs."

They both laugh. "We're very square," says the wife.

"You don't need to," Wolf says. "I don't need to, I got LSD in my blood. But I tried once. I ate some magic mushrooms and when I got up the next morning I saw angels the size of the Empire State Building dancing in front

of me. Then I saw fireworks. Here it is—everything I saw."

The couple studies "Psychedelic Dreams," nodding in a somewhat tepid turn-on.

Wolf shows the tourists a work he did in Israel based on the events at Masada in the 7th century when the remaining Jews of that besieged city committed suicide rather than surrender to the Romans. "This painting," says Wolf. "I don't sell."

However, for sale is "The Seven Wonders of the World." Wolf points out on the canvas, among a kaleidoscopic collage of other wonders, the Great Wall of China. "Too bad," he says, "it didn't fall down when Nixon was there."

The man and woman aren't smiling. Wolf shrugs. "You don't like that? Permit me my little joke."

They allow the artist his license, assure him that the guided gallery tour was very interesting and the woman adds she was "very impressed." In lieu of a sale, Wolf settles for the compliments.

"What I would really like," he says, "is that the gallery should be my dining room. I'd like to have my friends over and eat here with the paintings around us and maybe sell one a month.

"You know," he tells the reporter, "after they wrecked my gallery and the paintings, I didn't do anything for six weeks. I was feeling terrible. Eight years of paintings were ruined. I was broke. But then I decided, it's much more heroic to build from the shambles, than to give up. A man should never give up.

"That's the end of the article, isn't it?"

May 5, 1974

D.I. Wolf

Tony Tursi: Proud Owner of New 'Diploma'

The talk was of *habeas corpus, amicus curiae* and *writs of mandamus*. One could have been sitting across the desk from the president of the Bar Association. But one was not at the Bar Association. One was in La Riviera Club, interviewing Anthony J. (Tony) Tursi.

It was a big day for Tursi. "Graduation Day," you could say. It was Thursday, Dec. 16, 1982, the day on which Tony Tursi officially completed his eight-year sentence for tax evasion and possession of stolen airline tickets.

Tursi did not have his "diploma" yet. He went early that morning to visit his probation officer at the federal building in Hato Rey—he spent five years in prison and the last three on parole—and was told his release papers could not be handed over until midnight, and would be mailed to him. But for all intents and purposes, he was a free man—allowed, like the rest of us, to park his car on sidewalks, jaywalk and even be seen in nightclubs where prostitutes are said to congregate.

Tursi, of course, is the notorious and-or colorful fellow who operates just such a club. In 1968, he declared himself a write-in candidate for mayor of San Juan, and the news media, ever on the lookout for a candidate with a new approach, was more than happy to amply report on his campaign activities.

The New Progressive Party had Carlos Romero Barceló as candidate, the Popular Democratic Party had Jorge Font Saldaña. But the press had Tursi. While the rest of the candidates were hacking it along the same old campaign trail, Tursi and his team were moving and grooving. He called a news conference to inaugurate his waterfront clean-up campaign at which a dozen or so of his female employees appeared in short-shorts and with paint rollers to spruce up some buildings down on the docks. They rolled their rollers to rhythm provided by La Riviera's steel band.

Earlier, Tursi had been the man the Vice Squad loved to hate. In those days, whenever the fellows down at Vice were feeling particularly virtuous, which seemed in Tursi's case, about every week, they decided to raid a nightclub where prostitutes were said to congregate. But, like Big Julie of Chicago in "Guys and Dolls," Tursi was able to boast then that his record was clean—87 arrests and no convictions.

One of the raids resulted in the police apprehending several dozen mattresses from a nearby hotel where the prostitutes who were said to congregate at La Riviera were said to take their clients. Tursi got a court order and the police had to free the mattresses and bring them back to the site of their alleged crime.

Anyway, all those good old days, when Tony Tursi was a celebrity of sorts, are no longer with us. But their memories linger on the walls of his office. Framed up there are the stories of his campaign, and dozens of photos. Most of them are pictures of the yearly. Thanksgiving bash he used to throw at the club for poor kids.

Before his conviction when his persona became non grata, look who turned out for the parties. There's Mayor Felisa Rincon de Gautier sitting at the guest table with, among others, the young maverick senator, José Arsenio Torres. There's Roberto Clemente and Xavier Cugat and Kid Gavilan and Bobby Vinton and "Terin" Pizarro not to mention baseball great Johnny Bench and local comedian José Miguel Agrelot. There's Tursi sharing a table with José Ferrer. The candidate is shown visiting the lord mayor of London, conferring at a local discotheque with former New York Mayor Vincent Impellitteri.

Tursi has managed to stay out of the limelight during his parole, and says he will continue to keep his profile low. "Maybe that was cute years ago," he said recently of the celebrity life. "But I don't really miss it. It can be very, very prejudicial."

He is convinced that the authorities jumped on him to stamp out his notoriety. How else to explain that his original sentence was nine to 15 years for tax evasion. Pretty remarkable, Tursi says, since no one has ever served time in Puerto Rico for tax evasion, before or since. Except, that is, for another "continental", who reportedly got about four months a year before Tursi got his eight-year sentence on similar charges.

The Commonwealth Supreme Court lowered the sentence to three to five years. Another five years were added on for the stolen airline tickets conviction.

Tursi insists today he had nothing to do with stealing the tickets, nor did he buy them.

He spent three years at the Rio Piedras Penitentiary and two years at federal penitentiaries in Pennsylvania. He passed a test to become a law clerk in the prison library at Allenwood and wrote many a mandamus for fellow convicts. Among other things, he says, he wrote the writ that got former baseball star Orlando Cepeda's sentence cut, "after his attorneys failed." Cepeda's term was lowered from five years to a year on marijuana charges.

One of his biggest thrills, he said, was rewriting a brief for a prisoner which was originally prepared by a national figure-turned-convict.

"This kid was transferred to Allenwood from Alabama and he showed me this *habeas corpus.* I asked him who wrote it. He said a guy by the name of John Mitchell wrote it, citing wrong statutes in conferring jurisdiction. He should have attached a memorandum of law. I wrote to the court in Alabama, stating that I am now replacing (former Justice Secretary) Mitchell as representing the kid."

Tursi says he also represented more than 75 prisoners at parole hearings. "The Parole Board would tell the prisoner, 'You're being represented by Mr. Tursi, who is very knowledgeable.' That used to make me feel good."

His old boss at the Allenwood prison library still calls him, he said, to ask how to find projects Tursi had been working on. Tursi said he used to give law classes to other convicts.

When he was at the Rio Piedras Penitentiary, Tursi filed the suit that led to U.S. District Court Judge Juan A. Torruella visiting the prison. Tursi was one of the inmates who showed the judge around. "We insisted he see certain places that they (prison authorities) wouldn't have shown him. Like where they keep the nuts. And solitary. He, Torruella, came out of there a little green around the gills."

After the visit, Torruella ordered authorities to clean up their act there or close the place down. Tursi said the warden reacted by shutting him up for two weeks in the "Monoloro" solitary section, until a petition by 800 fellow inmates got him out.

Why doesn't Tony Tursi, born in Brooklyn 56 years ago, now become what he says he could be: a paralegal?

"Unfortunately," said Tursi, "at my age, how many years have I got left? I just want to try to live them out and enjoy myself. The law will only bog me down."

He added: "Forget about all the good things I do. All they are going to remember about me is that I ran a..."

Well, a club where prostitutes were said to congregate.

Dec. 19, 1982

Tony Tursi at the entrance to his night club.
(Photo by Tony Pacheco)

Women's—and
Some Men's—Lib

The "Woman's Lib" movement of the 1970s and 1980s wound its way to Puerto Rico, and both legally and attitudinally improved the status of island women, who no longer were strongly coaxed into sterilization, as they were as late as in the 1960s, or used as guinea pigs in early tests of The Pill. The movement led in 1973 to the creation of the Commission for the Improvement of Women's Rights, a government agency concerned with sex discrimination and domestic violence. Following the U.S. Supreme Court's Roe v. Wade decision, also in 1973, abortion was legalized on the island--even though the male-dominated Puerto Rican Senate has subsequently tried, unsuccessfully, to ban abortions for any reason other than a woman protecting her health.

In 1976, the family law was amended, giving women joint administration of assets accumulated after marriage, equalizing parental authority and allowing women to enter into contracts—all of which they presumably were not allowed before. In 1989, Law 54 was passed, criminalizing domestic violence, which before was prosecuted, though only occasionally, as regular assault.

Not that island women had been completely stilled on the political front during the 1960s through the 1980s. Felisa Rincón de Gautier, a.k.a. Doña Fela, the first woman ever elected as mayor in the capital city of the Americas (1948), was winding up her fifth term as San Juan mayor in 1968; Lolita Lebrón, pardoned in 1979 by President Carter after she spent 25 years in federal prison for shooting up Congress in 1954 (no deaths, was seen as, and listened to, by many *independentistas*, as a martyr for their cause; Miriam Ramírez de Ferrer, elected to the Island Senate in 1973, knew how to get the press to cover her many moves for Puerto Rico statehood.

Without trying to trivialize the plight of women in Puerto Rico down through the ages, here are a couple of articles I wrote in 1980 and 1984-the latter for the *San Juan Sun*, a short-lived publication put out by the striking staff of the *Star*--about my experience for the liberation of men, as far as the birth of their children were concerned.

Doña Felisa   **Lolita Lebron**   **Miriam Ramírez**

One Father's Labor Pains

A very ordinary thing happened to me the other day. It's happened to billions before me and, one hopes against hope, it will happen to billions upon billions more in the future.

At the ripe middle age of 46, I became, for the first time, a father! And I went through it—the coming of fatherhood—the way, any self-respecting dad who believes in men's lib should go through this thing. I was in the delivery room. I was here to stand beside my wife, hold her hand, sweat with her, and mop both our brows and urge her along with the doctors and nurses to push, push, p-u-u-u-sh!

I was there when my wife, Ginny—her face turning bright pink, then tomato red, then scarlet, then crimson—gave her heroic all in one last thrust down into the deepest reaches of her body and when through the blood, sweat and tears this little head silently popped out to the shoulders, gave a quick look around the room and, seeming not to like what it saw, closed its eyes, crunched up

its face and wailed to get back where it came from.

But, of course, seconds later the little creature was doomed to share with every other thing that was ever born: the unutterably sad knowledge that there was no turning back.

With a little help from a friend—Dr. Jorge García Padial—Madeline Friedman was born into what might not be the best of all possible worlds, but it's the only world we've got.

She came out purple with white vernix splotches. She was rested a few minutes on her mother's stomach, then taken over to a linen-lined metal tray. The nurses washed off the cream-like vernix that covers newborn babies and patted the soles of her feet and the palms of her hands and Madeline went from blue-purple to rosy pink, like the color developing on a Polaroid.

As I watched our baby being born, I wasn't taken so much with the "miracle" of birth, as by its complete naturalness. The miracle was what happened inside the womb—how do those tiny fingers and infinitesimal fingernails become so perfectly formed? But the birth, itself, seemed a simple, beautiful act of nature.

My wife was fortunate; she was in labor less than four hours. Other women giving birth for the first time are not nearly so lucky; their labor can, and often does, last 14, 18 or 20 hours. For many of these women, nature charges a heavy price for its show.

Which brings us to "prepared" childbirth and how women can minimize the pain, the fear and the trembling—and how husbands can get into the act —in a supporting role, anyway.

About three months before the due date, my wife and I took eight weekly classes—two hours a class—at the Ashford Memorial Community (Presbyterian) Hospital. The lessons were given by Joanne Burriss, a nurse-midwife, and Beth Geary, a registered nurse. Mrs. Burriss and her husband, Ray Burriss, run Family Centered Education, which gives prenatal classes to expectant mothers, and fathers.

What did I—an expectant daddy—learn? A hell of a lot more than I ever knew before about birthin' babies. I learned what's happening inside a women's body as the baby develops. I learned how to coach my wife in the breathing exercises she was taught to deflect the... "sensations" (we don't use the word, pain) of childbirth. I learned once again something you can't learn too many times: that fear comes from ignorance (I'm talking about my initial fear of being on the birth scene) and that knowledge—as well as love, faith and good intentions—helps us make it through the crucial times.

Prepared childbirth, for those unliberated fathers still into waiting rooms, is based on the Lamaze method, devised by the French obstetrician Fernand Lamaze in 1951 after he saw similar methods of childbirth being used in the Soviet Union. Its technical name is the psychoprophylactic method of childbirth, which aims to prevent or lessen pain by psychological and physical means.

Actually, the pioneer in the whole process was an English doctor, Grantly Dick-Read, who came up with the idea in the 1930's that pain during labor was caused primarily by fear. He wrote that such pain could be greatly reduced when women understood the process of labor and delivery and learned to relax properly.

The first half of each class is devoted to lectures about the changes taking place inside the mother during gestation. During the second half, the women are taught the exercises and breathing techniques meant to prime their bodies and relax their psyches for easing the—excuse the expression—pain, and the anxiety during labor and delivery.

Papi kneels beside his wife, calling out the timing of simulated contractions and making sure she is relaxing as she practices her breathing techniques, each devised to more or less keep in rhythm with the strength and frequency of the contractions. There is homework too: practicing what was learned in class.

No one connected with Family Centered Education ignores the strain and stress and hard work of childbirth. What they manage to do, however, is to make you understand just what the birth process entails. By understanding it, you can turn the anticipated grim and grisly into a really happy high. And you don't get that way on drugs, because the method plays down the use of them—although it recognizes the need in certain circumstances.

It should also be noted that even if women go through these classes, some may still have to have a Caesarean section. According to Mrs. Burriss, who has attended thousands of births in Puerto Rico, the overwhelming majority of doctors here only perform that operation for what they consider compelling medical reasons.

Prepared childbirth is catching on in the states and, to some degree, in Puerto Rico. Top-notch doctors like García Padial, and several others, are all for it. And—amazingly— even some hospitals are showing signs of acknowledging that the wishes of expectant mothers, and fathers, are as important as the convenience of the hospital staff. Ashford Memorial, where my wife gave birth, now has a special psychoprophylactic clinic with smaller, almost homey, certainly less alienating-looking, labor and delivery rooms for those who took prepared child-birth classes. The clinic is staffed by nurses trained in the method.

The idea is for mom and pop to keep asking hospitals to do more things that will make childbirth a more humanizing experience. As it now stands, no hospital here allows the baby to stay in the mother's room, as is being done in some hospitals in the states and many in Europe. But if enough parents tell their doctors that's what they want, the doctors could get the word to the hospitals, which could, perhaps reluctantly, get into the swing of things to come.

Here's hoping more and more expectant fathers also get into the swing of being there when their babies are born. It's a great, liberating experience, fellas.

Sept. 30, 1980

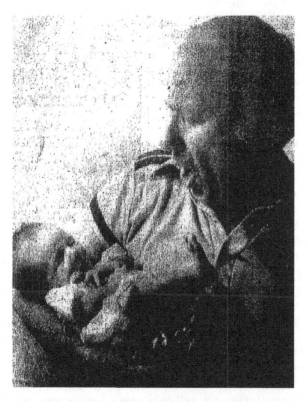

Liberated father Robert Friedman and daughter Madeline. (*Star* photo by Rafael H. Trios)

The Days of Elizabeth

Come Christmas, Elizabeth will be two months old. She came into this world on the night of Oct. 25, weighing 2 pounds 9 ounces. Like all newborns, her weight soon dropped. After she was transferred on the night of her birth at Ashford Community Hospital to San Juan Municipal Hospital, she barely tipped the scales at 2 pound 4 ounces.

Elizabeth was a premature baby, arriving some seven weeks before her time. Everything was in place—eyes, ears, nose, mouth, toes, infinitesimal fingernails. But, frankly, this little newborn, with her dry, yellowish complexion, baggy eyes, drooping cheeks and drawn-in mouth, looked not unlike an incredibly shrunken 105-year-old crone.

The first 48 to 72 hours after birth, the doctors said, would be crucial. Elizabeth soon developed an infection and the doctors told her parents not to get their hopes up too high for her survival.

Elizabeth did survive the first 72 hours and fought off the infection. But, for her parents at least, one crucial period ended just in time for the following one to begin.

Next came the seizures, probably brought on by hemorrhaging in the brain. The doctors said not to worry—yet. Such "episodes" were fairly common among "preemies." There would be tests, C-T scans, EEGs and sonograms to assess brain damage, if any, a test for possible meningitis. An explanation was given as to what degree of hemorrhaging could bring on encephalitis. The father prodded the worst possible scenarios from the doctors, then converted them in his brain into impending reality.

The doctors found no apparent brain damage. Elizabeth began improving, taking milk through a tube and gaining weight. Then, she was hit with another infection. Her heartbeat slowed dangerously. For the first time, she was put on a respirator. One more tube, this one down her throat, joined the other tubes and the wires on or in her nose, head, chest, arms, legs.

The doctor told the parents, the life of this very little person was now in the hands of God.

The systems of premature babies are so immature, the parents learned, that the condition of these babies may change in the shortest span from stable to highly critical to stable and back and forth again. So the stomach tightened and the nerves went taut at each day's visit and each evening's phone call to the nursery. One day everything is fine. The parents' spirits are up. The next day, the rollercoaster plunges.

Elizabeth overcame her second infection. In the past few weeks, it has been two steps forward for every one backward. New words have come into the parents' vocabulary. Such as "apnea," a condition in which premature babies "forget" to breathe for 15 seconds or so. Nothing to worry too much about, unless the apnea brings on "bradicardia," a slowing down of the heartbeat. Elizabeth, like many preemies, has had a couple of apnea episodes.

Premature babies help parents put things in perspective. You'd be surprised how unimportant it suddenly became who would govern Puerto Rico or be president of the United States for the next four years, compared to the outcome of that gigantic struggle being waged in near-silence by the diminutive creature inside her incubator.

At her last weigh-in, Elizabeth was "up" to 3 pounds 8 ounces. Her complexion has turned almost rosy. Awake, she stares straight into your eyes, grabs your finger and—her parents insist—smiles.

When people learn that you have had a premature baby, they regale you with stories of preemies they have known who are now 6-foot-tall bone-crushers. Books tell you that Winston Churchill, Charles Darwin and Albert Einstein, among others, were premature babies.

My daughter, Elizabeth Friedman, it now appears, will survive. No small thanks are due the doctors and nurses of the Municipal Hospital's intensive-care nursery. They are a mostly young and incredibly dedicated staff who work long and hard hours.

Her parents probably will pull through also to celebrate a Christmas in which the cascade of written and spoken words about the spirit of the season actually takes on meaning.

Nov. 9, 1984

Carpetas, COINTELPRO and Other Un-American Activities

*T*hey were called *carpetas* (files), and there were more than 150,000 of them— some 75,000 on individuals, others on the organizations they belonged to, as well as information about their vehicles and boats and the island towns where they lived. The island's police had been compiling the *carpetas* on "political subversives" since the 1930s. When the police files came to light in 1987 a lot of angry Puerto Ricans whose names were in the files went to the courts, which ruled that the files should be turned over to the individuals and the names of their informants disclosed.

For the *carpeta* compilers just about all the so-called subversives were on the list because they supported independence for the island. The island police had help over the years from the feds in the hunt for the perceived political radicals. Meanwhile, the FBI decided to get into the anti-*independentista* act in the Sixties, when it began to apply its Counter Intelligence Program (COINTELPRO), which originally was

meant to rout out communists, to the independence movement in both Puerto Rico and the states.

(At a House hearing in 2000, then-FBI Director Louis Freeh
acknowledged that the FBI had been keeping these dossiers on
independence supporters. The agency began releasing the first
few thousand of what it said were the 1.8 million documents
it had on island activities. In an early COINTELPRO memo on
Puerto Rico, dated Aug. 5 1960, FBI Director J. Edgar Hoover
told the San Juan office: "The Bureau is considering the fea-
sibility of instituting a program of disruption to be directed
against organizations which seek independence for Puerto
Rico through other than peaceful means." He said that "mere
harassment" wasn't enough and suggested using "carefully se-
lected informants" in the independence groups and planting
disinformation stories in the island press.

The memo, along with other documents and articles
about political surveillance, harassment and suppression on
the island, is reprinted in the book, *Las Carpetas. Persecución
política y derechos civiles en Puerto Rico* (The Files. Political
Persecution and Civil Rights in Puerto Rico).

Then came the federal Grand Jury investigations into independence groups, like FALN, which have been accused of terrorism. Several of those called were *independentistas* who refused to
testify. They were given prison terms. Among them was Carlos
Noya Murati, then 28, who was put away in a federal pen for 34
months, almost three years, because he refused to tell what he
knew about FALN's operations, which he later said was nothing. His refusal to testify to a U.S. Grand Jury is against the law,
but given the harassment of independence supporters down
through the years, many may wonder if that is truly a crime.

Carlos Noya, Home Again, Feels Victorious

Carlos Noya III, picks up a video cassette of "Amadeus" and toddles over to the VCR. "Watch this," says his proud father. He turns the cassette around for the boy, who deftly slides it into the loader, closes the lid, pushes a few buttons. You recognize the flush to the father's face—a sign of the rush to the heart over the accomplishment of his 18-month-old son.

"He was two weeks old when I entered prison. I'm trying to re-establish our relationship. Slowly but surely."

The father is Carlos Noya Murati, 31 years of age. Before his release last Monday, he had spent 34 months of his last five years in federal prisons on two 17-month terms because he refused to testify twice before grand juries—one in San Juan, the other in Brooklyn. A fervent *independentista*, he refused to tell the panels what, if anything, he knew about activities of the FALN violent separatist organization.

He is home now, in his parents' house, where he was raised, in the non-radical, middle-class section of Miramar. He sits in a rocking chair next to a Christmas tree and surrounded by his son's Fisher-Price toys.

His wife, Lourdes Santana, 29, sits next to him. She is one of the "Vieques 21," brought to trial in 1979 for trespassing in a demonstration against the Navy on the offshore island. She says she is "happy and proud" to have her husband home again. After Noya Murati was jailed for the second time, she and the baby moved in with his parents.

His mother, Irmahé Murati de Noya, sits across from him. She says her son's return is "the best Christmas present I have had in my whole life."

His sister, Diana, who came down from New York for the return, is in the kitchen, preparing food for a friend. His father, Dr. Carlos Noya and another sister, Laura, are attending patients in the dental offices they share just a few blocks from the family home.

You could say Noya Murati had been locked up for nearly three years of his young life despite not having committed any crime, other than refusing to help federal law enforcement

157

authorities do their job. (Noya says he couldn't have helped anyway because he knows nothing about FALN activities. He refused to cooperate with the grand juries because of his pro-independence principles.)

You could say that since Noya never has been charged with or linked to any FALN acts, a grave injustice has been committed against him. You also could say that in a democracy people are not supposed to be put in jail for nearly three years without being charged with serious crimes, that in a democracy you don't lock up political dissidents for what they do, or do not, say.

The irony is that many people who are neither anti-American nor pro-independence seem more upset than Noya over his treatment by the federal system.

"I don't feel angry, or frustrated, over what happened," he said the other day. "I feel... victorious. I established the fact that I would not collaborate with the grand jury. I fought against the growing tendency of the U.S. government to eliminate the civil and human rights gained before, and I protected the struggle for independence.

"I feel that I have fulfilled my responsibility as a Puerto Rican and as a father because I

did nothing that my son will be ashamed of."

His future, he said, is still somewhat up in the air. He would like to be able to work and study. He has completed two years of university studies and wants to get a degree in political science. He also works as a cabinetmaker. "I was an apprentice when I went into prison, but now I'm skilled. But, it wasn't the prison that taught me. It was my fellow-prisoners," he says with a gentle smile.

Everything seems gentle about Noya Murati—even when he talks to you about his "feeling of solidarity with the oppressed," and "the damage that the capitalistic system does to the people of the world," and the interests of "the Pentagon and the multi-nationals in keeping Puerto Rico a colony." When he talks about politics, his eyes shine and you sense the True Believer, for whom the complexities of the human condition will be forever simplified by the true application of Marxist dialectic. But overall is the feeling of gentleness.

His father, a founding member of the New Progressive Party, had been a true believer, of sorts, himself. He believed strongly in the American way of life, liberty and justice. His belief in American justice now appears diminished. The elder Noya has picketed the U.S. District Court in Old San Juan 75 times, almost every Friday, since his son was sent to jail for a second time.

He said the other day of his son's release: "I'm elated, not only because he is home, but because he is out of prison, where he did not belong.

"I was at the prison (in Tallahassee, Fla.) Monday when they released him, and I was there on July 16, 1984 when he went in. Both times I felt sad. But the second time it was a different sadness, over what he had been put through without justification."

Noya was also happy on that second occasion, because his son came out of prison, "with his head high and his spirit unbroken. That is what I admire most about him." said his father. "He is a person who acts according to his principles and ideals. He didn't give in. They did not break him."

You recognize the flush to the face as a sign of the rush to the heart.

Dec. 30, 1987

The Media

*T*he news media was alive, well and occasionally over the top or off the deep end during my time on the island. Newspapers generally thrived—if one closed down, another opened soon after, and the local airwaves were filled with news broadcasts and political punditry.

The three most important dailies during those years were *El Mundo, El Nuevo Día* and the English-language *San Juan Star*, all of which more or less upheld the journalistic principles of fairness and accuracy. They also engaged from time to time in investigative reporting, as well as issuing a myriad of opinion pieces on the island's political, social and economic life. The *Star* won a Pulitzer Prize in 1961—the only Puerto Rico newspaper to have received such an honor—and it deserved one in the Seventies for its investigative reporting on the cover-up after the Cerro Maravilla killings. Of the three, only *El Nuevo Día* is still publishing.

The pro-independence *Claridad*, which is still being put out weekly, brought the Marxist-Leninist point of view to readers, while *El Imparcial* was the leading daily crime sheet, until it closed down in 1973. Much of the newspaper's staff then went to work for the new *El Vocero*, which still publishes daily and now is distributed freely. The short-lived

El Reportero (1980-1987) was a strong supporter of the Commonwealth status.

Some strange things happened in newspaper city rooms, which like most island offices, were easy to access then. One day, an inebriated reader entered the *San Juan Star* building, ignored the operator in her booth on the ground floor and climbed to the second floor where the news offices were located. He demanded to see the editor. He was wielding a machete.

Editor Andy Viglucci happened to be in the newsroom at the time and went over to the man, who was protesting about something, the machete waving in his hand. Viglucci listened, stood his ground and suggested that the man put away the machete. The guy put the machete in the leather sheath on his belt. They continued talking. The guy nodded to another suggestion about writing a letter to the editor and left the office.

Another day in the newsroom.

Among the many radio and TV programs analyzing political and status happenings, real or imagined, was the popular *Cara a Cara Ante el Pais* (Face to Face Before the Country), whose weekly panels included the island's top politicians, journalists, commentators, analysts, and other talking heads.

Most of the leading U.S. mainland newspapers in cities where a significant number of Puerto Ricans settled over the years had special correspondents on the island. They usually were local journalists moonlighting for the U.S. publications. Journalists also visited from around the world to report on the Caribbean's "Showcase of Democracy," and for other stories. Here is one of those "other" stories, very far from earth-shaking, that brought some British reporters to Puerto Rico.

It's Really Quite Cricket to Hound Royalty

It is 7 a.m., the sun is up, rashers of bacon and eggs have been served and—tally ho!—it is time to follow the hounds. The hunt is on!

Actually, the leaders of the hunt are of the *canis newshoundis* family, trained in the pits of London's Fleet Street to mercilessly track down their special prey; the royal family.

Two rented, air-conditioned cars leave the Caribe Hilton parking lot to give chase to the quarry. Mounted in one of the vehicles are Baz Bamigboye of the *London Sun* (circulation 4.2 million), David Bradbury of the *London Daily Mirror* (circulation 3.2 million) and George Gordon of the *London Daily Mail* (circulation 1.9 million.)

The second car carries photographers to pictorially record the catch for the combined readership of 9.3 million British commoners, on tenterhooks for the next episode of the escapades of Prince Andrew of Great Britain, better known outside the grounds of Buckingham Palace as Randy Andy.

The prince is sailing the Caribbean aboard HMS Invincible, an aircraft carrier taking part in NATO maneuvers in these waters. As a helicopter pilot in Her Majesty's (his mother's) Navy, Andrew is participating in the exercises. He is also working out in other areas, having been spied by Bamigboye, Bradburry and Gordon in Barbados with three young women, taking a dip in the surf "au naturel."

Andrew in the altogether was front-page news in the London tabloids, of course. Royal-watching has become a fever in Britain with London's 10 major dailies and eight major Sunday papers reportedly "jostling brashly for sensation and circulation" (Time; Feb. 28, 1983) on the latest comings and goings-on of the House of Windsor.

And now Prince Andrew was in Puerto Rico for 24 hours and three British reporters—all of whom are the New York correspondents for their newspapers—were, well, not quite jostling brashly. Actually, they were riding together in the same car, along with a British reporter-watching acquaintance, sharing stories and jokes and admiring the countryside on the way to Roosevelt Roads Naval Station on the eastern end of the island, where the prince's ship was set to dock.

The intensity of royal family-watching really took off when "Shy Di"—the new princess Diana—came on the scene, said Bradbury of the *Mirror*. "It's a new phenomenon, the way it's going on now," he said. "It's more about the personal side of their lives."

Is it really cricket to subject the royal family to such intense scrutiny by the news media? You bet your bottom farthing, said Gordon, Bradbury and Bamigboye.

"The royal family essentially are public relations people," said Bradbury. "They're out on show, on a brutal political level, to maintain their position. They have to be on show, and be nice people, to keep their jobs."

Bamigboye added: "It all comes down to this; What are they there for? If you can't report on them, why are they there? What is a queen for? To be seen."

But why does the British press put in so much time and effort and money (Bamigboye said that he has spent about $20,000 chasing the prince around the Caribbean), why all these resources to come up with such. . . well, trivia?

Now if you asked such a question to an American journalist, you would get answers involving the First Amendment and the people's right to know and other similar sentiments. When you ask such a question to British journalists, you get this answer; Because, old chap," it sells newspapers."

"You have a 23-year-old kid, slightly irresponsible, (Prince Andrew), having an affair with a soft-porn actress (Kathleen 'Ko' Stark), showing his naked bum to the world—it's all good fun," said Bamigboye. "It's fun to write about and it's fun to read."

So the dirty little secret is out. Yes, journalism can be fun. For the reporters as well as the readers. Sometimes, even, for the subjects themselves, The British seem to be aware of this. Their journalists seldom take themselves seriously, as New World practitioners of the trade often do. Which doesn't mean that journalists cannot accomplish serious things. But realize the limitations, old chaps, and loosen up.

Anyway, back on the trail of the prince. As readers of the *San Juan Star* know, the press was turned back at the gates of

Roosevelt Roads, and Andrew went unwatched in Puerto Rico.

Riding back from the naval base, the reporters passed a cock-fighting arena. "That's the picture we need," said Bradbury, "Andrew at a cockfight; his eyes suffused with blood lust! With that we can all go home happy."

They went home happy anyway.

Feb. 27, 1983

(Editor's note: The above-mentioned Prince Andrew is he who has recently lost the backing of the British Royal Family due to recent disclosures of past sexual shenanigans with underage females.)

Write On

*J*ournalism, as the saying goes, is the first (often rough) draft of history. The last word usually is found in the literary works of a people: the novels, short stories, plays, memoirs, essays. Where do we learn the most about life in Victorian English society if not in the novels of Dickens, or about 19th Century Russia—how about the "fiction" of Dostoyevsky and Tolstoy, the plays and short stories of Chekhov?

Probably nothing written gives a more heartfelt picture of what life was like in Vieques during the U.S. Navy's occupation of the island than Pedro Juan Soto's novel, *Usmail;* of how bizarre is much of modem-day island society than Luis Rafael Sánchez's *La Guaracha del Macho Camacho,* or what it means to go through the culture clashes of being Puerto Rican in New York than Esmeralda Santiago's *When I Was Puerto Rican.*

Several well-known writers made Puerto Rico home for a while in the 1960s, 70s or 80s. They included Nobel Prize winners Saul Bellow and Mario Vargas Llosa, "gonzo" journalist Hunter S. Thompson, and Pulitzer Prize-winning novelist William Kennedy, who also happened to be the first managing editor of the *San Juan Star.* Kennedy moved back to his Albany, N.Y. hometown in 1962, but visited the island often in the following years. His wife, dancer-actress Dana Sosa, was born in Ponce

A special word about a special writer and a good friend, Edgardo Vega Yunqué, who before he died in 2008 wrote three captivating and fierce novels about Puerto Ricans in New York. The first two went by very long titles: *No Matter How Much You Promise to Cook or Pay the Rent You Blew It Cause Bill Bailey Ain't Never Coming Home Again,* and *The Lamentable Journey of Omaha Bigelow Into the Impenetrable Loisaida Jungle.* His third big novel was *Blood Fugues.*

Ed and I met twice in New York. We communicated often by email. I found him kind, sensitive, vulnerable, bitterly sweet, a little paranoid, intensely intelligent and incredibly generous. He wrote a great blurb for my novel, *Shadow of the Fathers* (retitled *The Odyssey of Pablo Camino*), and asked on his own to read it before it was published, then volunteered to edit it, at which he did a great job. We had a few disagreements. Ed thought that Hugo Chávez was a Godsend for Venezuela and all Latin Americans, while cynical me said God save us from all saviors, political or otherwise.

Although most of Ed's kudos came for *Bill Bailey,* which probably is his most profound work, my favorite is *Omaha Bigelow* in all its magic realism, raunchiness and resonance about the Nuyoricans of the Lower East Side. Ed, always on the lookout to rile-up readers, intervenes post-modernly in the novel with opinions on art, life, literature and, especially, the U.S.-Puerto Rico relationship. He was always highly critical of the U.S. government for its treatment of the island, but he was 100 percent New Yorker who knew cruelty and evil when he saw it. In the book's finale, Omaha Bigelow, the sympathetic punk-rock Gringo loser, is literally turned into a monkey and exiled into a real jungle for his unfaithfulness by his 15-year-old Puerto Rican girlfriend, who also happens to be a *bruja* (a witch). All this comes about shortly after the attack on the Twin Towers. Here's how the novel ends:

"When Omaha Bigelow felt particularly lonely, he climbed to the top of the very highest tree in the jungle, and from there he scanned the horizon and saw the vastness of the sea, its surface shimmering blue and emerald in the brilliant sunlight. If he concentrated more diligently, he could make himself look beyond the sea, and in his memory he was back in the East Village, standing on the rooftop of a building in the projects. From that vantage point he could look southward. He didn't know why, but his heart ached when he saw the empty spaces of his mind where the towers had been. He could not explain their absence, but in his mind they were gone. He didn't know what had happened, but he knew that something had taken place that was surrounded by horror. He thought that perhaps it was his own failed life that saddened him. Tears came into his eyes, and he knew he would never be happy again. He was just a poor monkey mired in the complexity of a world that had lost its poetry. Perhaps, he thought in his muddled monkey mind, we are all poor confused monkeys and all of us are lost in a world devoid of poetry."

The following articles feature an interview with Kennedy and with one of Puerto Rico's bright literary lights in the 1960s, Piri Thomas, a "Neuyorican" who often visited the island. Esmeralda Santiago and Edgardo Vega Yunqué, both island-born and New York-raised, were interviewed after I left the island to live and work for the *Star* in Washington, D.C.

Kennedy Went Home to Find Sense of Place

William Kennedy, 56, who has staked out turf in Albany, N.Y. as his literary capital, was talking the other day about "sense of place," and its importance to writers everywhere.

Take, for instance, William Faulkner, whose characters were inextricably intertwined with the fictitious Yoknapatawpha County, which was really Faulkner's hometown of Oxford, Mississippi, Or Ernest Hemingway, who was vividly at home away from home in Paris, Madrid and Havana. Or James Joyce. "Where is Joyce without Dublin? That city was the crucible for his imagination."

And where would Bill Kennedy and the city of Albany be without one another?

Kennedy has put New York state's political capital on the literary map by showing its all-too-human side. And the town where politicians have controlled life "down to the pigeons in the gutter" has spurred Bill Kennedy, a native of that city, onwards and upwards into the literary firmament. His Albany Cycle ("Legs," Billy Phelan's Greatest Game" and "Ironweed") has won him awards, wide publicity and screen writing contracts.

"Ironweed" took the prestigious National Book Critics Circle award last January as best fiction book of 1983 (and the 1984 Pulitzer Prize for Fiction) Kennedy received last year a MacArthur Foundation Award, which gives him $256,000 over five years to do with as he may; he is working on the script of Francis Ford Coppola's latest film, "Cotton Club," as well as writing the movie versions of his Albany trilogy.

While Albany is now where it's at for Kennedy, it is not where he has always been. He spent six years in San Juan (1956-63, interrupted by a year in Miami), where he wrote short stories and two unpublished novels and toiled at local journalism. He was assistant managing editor for the short-lived *World Journal* and the first managing editor of the *Star*. He married the dancer Dana Sosa, a New York Puerto Rican, helped bring up two of their three children here and has often come back for visits.

On a visit here last week, Kennedy called his Puerto Rico years "remarkably full and wonderful. It seemed as though the whole world was coming to Puerto Rico in those days," he said. "I interviewed Jack Kennedy and Rita Hayworth, among others. They probably visited Albany too, but it wasn't the same. Getting involved in the days of Operation Bootstrap was really exciting.

"And I was also involved in starting *two* newspapers here! How many journalists ever get the opportunity to be in on the beginning of just one newspaper?"

Yes, Kennedy admitted, journalism is still inextricably intertwined with his being. "I still look at the world as a good story," he said.

And when it comes to good stories, the "single most fascinating" one that has ever come out of the island, he believes, is the *Cerro Maravilla* case. He sees it as a deep personal tragedy and as a dramatic unfolding of fate.

"The extraordinary coverup and corruption of the police, the willful murder of two young people over a political issue that clearly didn't warrant that, the gradual escalation of involvement... I've followed it with the same interest that I followed Watergate," he said.

"The most striking thing about it, it seems to me, is that the evolution of justice is working, though it can never really work totally. But in this case, the persistence of the principal figures—the journalists, Pedro Juan (Soto, the author and father of one of the victims and a friend of Kennedy's), the people who believed in a conspiracy—has been admirable. I'm glad that the press played such an important role."

Yes, Kennedy said, *Cerro Maravilla* could be the stuff that great novels, or movies, are made of; no, he is not the one to write about it. "But I think someone should do it."

Not only did Kennedy's journalistic career take off in Puerto Rico, but he began writing fiction seriously here too. He met and was encouraged by Saul Bellow, when Bellow was teaching at the University of Puerto Rico. Bellow has been a Kennedy champion over the years. The Nobel Prize winner made the observation in an article about Kennedy that talent can go so far. "Then character takes over." He was referring to the way Kennedy stuck to novel writing through many lean years.

"You've got to be persistent," Kennedy said. "You have to refuse to accept failure as an alternative. If you just don't quit, you have a chance."

When Kennedy began to delve seriously into novel writing, he realized that his fictional truths awaited him back home.

"I had left Albany because I felt constricted. I was dying of boredom. It was an old man's town. I needed some vibrancy in my life." But he became aware that in Puerto Rico "I didn't have any depth, except journalistic depth. I was working out of a shallow comprehension of the language and the culture. If I wrote fiction about Puerto Rico, I would be at best a voyeur of Puerto Rican history... You have to put in a lot of time to get the dynamics of a place."

So he returned to his roots to interrelate people and place by writing about gangster Jack "Legs" Diamond, upon whom he bestowed a Gatsbyish aura in the Albany of the 1920s; and about Billy Phelan, a fictional character caught up in the real and ruthless world of 1930s Albany politics; and about Francis Phelan, Billy's fictional father, on the bum in Albany of Depression year 1938.

Francis Phelan is the protagonist of "Ironweed." It is a fine and beautiful novel about death and about life on the fringes and about guilt and expiation. It vibrates with unsentimental compassion. It takes into consideration the collapse of human lives, a consideration which is in such short supply nowadays among the nation's leaders.

Bill Kennedy is a writer not only with a sense of a particular place, but with a sensibility for the human condition in any place.

April 1, 1984

William Kennedy

Piri Thomas: 'Mean Streets' to Life's Open Road

As college campuses go, Inter American University in Hato Rey is not one of your vine-covered, shady green things. No stately palms or quiet enclave of buildings far from the mean traffic streets of the city. Instead, over-crowded, undersized, jerry-built classrooms rattled from time to time with descending jumbo jets or the frenetic fuming of all-day *tapones* (traffic jams). No House of Studies atmosphere here. More of a vibrant public housing project ambiance.

A high level of energy seems to vibrate through the packed hallways. No small college town sleepiness is evident, as at the University of Puerto Rico between riots. Too many students in too small a space, but IAU at Hato Rey has the lively air of an inner-city university and its students seem to have had at least some experience of the inner parts of the cities of San Juan and New York.

All of which makes close to an ideal setting for guest speaker Piri Thomas, who has experienced the innards of the city himself while being born in and branded by the heart of the heart of East Harlem, known as *El Barrio*.

Thomas is the former gang rumbler-drug addict-armed robber-prison con who broke out into the world of letters in 1967 with the publication of *Down These Mean Streets*, in which he dug into his own innards to bring forth a soul-searing account of his life on the streets and in prison. He has since followed up with two more books, *Savior, Savior, Hold My Hand* and *Seven Long Times*, but it is with "Mean Streets" that Thomas established his rep. It was a breakthrough book; with it Thomas became the first Puerto Rican writer to gain a wide audience in the States. He has even had the distinction of having the book banned, along with works by Kurt Vonnegut and Bernard Malamud, by the cultural commissars of Levittown, Long Island, and in other white, middle-class places like Darien, Conn. and Flushing in Queens.

So there before a standing-room-only audience of Puerto Rican students who are reaching for the Americanized Puerto

Rican dream through the portals of higher education stood Piri Thomas, who had spent seven long ones in Sing Sing and Comstock after wounding a policeman in a shoot-out during a robbery and who had, with an incredible act of will, come out through those portals a more human being who taught himself to turn around his nightmare existence.

He spoke for almost two hours, switching from English to Spanish to English to Spanish and back again, throwing in a little Yiddish, French, Italian and Hungarian, moving from pungent street talk to sermon-like revelational talk, shimmying shoulders and undulating fingers and hands, Sylvia del Villard-like, to bring softly curved drama to the point he was making. He was funny, incisive, shrewd, inspirational. There was wisdom in his cliches and cliches in his wisdom. He was entertaining as hell.

He remembers his teachers telling little brown-skinned, poverty-bred Piri Thomas, "Hey, stop talking that chica-chica-chic. You have to speak English. How else can you become president of the United States?" Or his mom telling him about these alley cats whose territory was invaded one day by this bad-ass

dog and the dog chased them down through the alleys Piri Thomas drew out their screeching cats' meows—and then one day the cats turned on the dog—Piri Thomas woofed out their quickly learned ferocious barks—"and the dog turned and ran like hell. And then my mom said, 'You see the importance of a second language'?"

He read from his poetry which was filled with images of the mean El Barrio streets and talked about the "incredible abnormality" of life in prison. He told of fighting to keep from becoming institutionalized, of the dangers of falling into homosexuality "if you're not strong enough. I went into prison my father and mother's son and I'd be damned if I would come out their daughter." One way he survived was by "sending my mind back to the Barrio at night."

Piri Thomas said, as he was to say over and over that morning, repeating what has become the leitmotif of his life: "It's all in your mind. You are what you think you are. No one can make you anything different from what you think you are."

He told how he changed "the negative of prison into a positive" through his relationship with other Puerto Rican prisoners.

"They (the prison authorities) tried to institutionalize us, make us into numbers, but we didn't let them because we recognized one another as Puerto Ricans. We all adopted names of places on the island. We saluted each other, "Hey, Santurce, Hey, Ponce. What's happening, Bayamón?"

Piri Thomas says, "I've learned to look back at the past without pain. You cannot have a future if you're stuck in a past of pain. As I get older—I'm 48 now—I get more clarity of vision. I have been there. I've fought with people. I've shot people. And I never did it to do it. I did it because I was enraged.

"I've been through the dogmatic ideologies, the corrupted politics and the commercialized religions. I decided I would rise above them all and look objectively at them. They all say, 'My road is the only road.' Well, I can only speak for me, Piri Thomas, and my road is creativity."

Questions from the floor. What is he working on at present? A book of poetry, a novel and a Broadway musical.

What is his opinion of American assimilation in Puerto Rico? "I don't mind learning from others as long as they don't try to turn me into one of them."

Yes, says the young woman who asked the question, but what is his *opinion* of the assimilation?

Words to the effect: "You who were born in Puerto Rico and live here, you know who you are. We (New York Puerto Ricans) never did. We got our image of Puerto Rico second-hand, from our family."

The young woman persists. What is his opinion, his moral judgement on American influence in Puerto Rico?

Piri Thomas launches into a very funny story about getting his hair straightened as a youngster and after he finishes convulsing the audience the young woman says, yes, but what is his *opinion* of the American presence on the island?

He knows what she's trying to get him to talk about and by this time she must know that he knows and that he doesn't want to get drawn into an ideological bag filled with hot polemic. But, finally, he relents some and says:

"If you want to talk about assimilation, we have it all over the world. Yes, I have a strong impression of U.S. influence in Puerto Rico. I think it's all right, if you can deal with it."

As a parting shot, Thomas, whose talk was sponsored by the IAU English Department, tells the students: "As a kid, I didn't mind learning English. I just resented being forced to learn it without being given a choice."

***

Cut to El Kiosko delicatessen where Thomas, his wife Betty, about 10 English Department professors and this reporter adjourn for lunch. Up close, Piri Thomas comes on very strong. He has not yet left the stage. The pearls of wisdom drop like the sweat coming from the brow of the reporter who begins to feel perhaps he shouldn't be here at all, that the story would have ended on a much neater note had he left after the talk at the university.

"My enemy," says Piri Thomas, apropos of the reporter is no longer sure what, "is not any one color. My enemy is a breed called greed."

Among other statements in no longer remembered—if any—contexts:

"I am what I am, I'm Popeye, the sailor man. Yo ask me for my experience, I give it to you. I'm Juanito Appleseed."

"I am an artist. I am a writer. You give me a word, I'll give you a symphony. When I write, I am giving birth. My babies are born with wings. I'm a dreamer, a poet. I see the future."

"They say I'm the first Puerto Rican to be this or that. I'm not the first. Pedro Juan Soto was the first when he wrote "Spiks," Julia de Burgos was the first with her beautiful poetry. I'm not the first, I just have the honor of being one of the beauties. There are lots of us—painters, poets, novelists, but we're not getting published. "Don't call us, we'll call you; the publishers say. 'You've seen one story about Puerto Ricans, you've seen them all," they say. They're so arrogant. Meanwhile, they're publishing the same old crap over and over. Other ethnic groups get more books published about us than we get published ourselves."

"When I was a kid someone called me nigger for the first time I went home to look up the word in a dictionary and I saw, 'niggardly, stingy,' and I went back and busted that kid in the mouth. No one was going to call me stingy."

"The PSP (Puerto Rican Socialist Party) wanted to drag me into their struggle so much. But I couldn't go with the rhetoric, man."

"Even as a child I was a poet laureate, an artist. I would go to church and kneel and make believe I was praying, but I was really only there to steal the candles so I could draw murals on the walls."

At about this juncture, Piri Thomas, song writer, leaned across the table to recite to four female Puerto Rican English teachers the opening lyrics of his latest hoped-for hit: "Ah sweet love, ah sweet love, there is really nothing like sweet love." The women giggled.

"I am childlike. Not childish, but *child-like*."

"The first beauty I ever saw in my life was when I came to Puerto Rico for the first time. I was 28. All I saw as a kid was the filth in the streets. My first day here, I almost drowned. I dove into the water and it was so beautiful down there I didn't want to come up."

"One of the hardest things was to have people here tell me I wasn't Puerto Rican. I said, 'Hey, don't you read your Bible? The prodigal son'. "

"Give me your respect, I'll give you mine. But if you don't, I'll blow your head off. But I am not a violent man."

"There's only one culture that is permanent and that's children. I **really** believe that. Children are the most beautiful thing on the earth, and most of the time we lie to them. They're pure energy and we pervert it. They become what they are taught."

"My writing is not obscene. I use the words of the streets. They're Anglo-Saxon words. They're not my words."

"You're your own warden, your own guard, your own prison. And you also have the key to open up the gates."

"I love America, but what makes it ugly is its lack of respect for the views of others."

"I hate the word, neorican. It's the same as nigger, kike, spic or wop. Neorican limits me to a place, a condition. But wherever my feet are, that's my turf. Can you understand? I'm tired of semantics. I've only felt a stranger in the face of racism. People make such a thing out of ethnic differences and they f—away humanity. If I can feel my humanity, I can have confidence being a Puerto Rican here or New York or anywhere in the world."

April 19. 1977

Piri Thomas

175

'When I Was Puerto Rican' Author a Hit

She grew up in a zinc shack in the Toa Baja countryside and in a house on stilts along the foul Martin Pena Charinel in Santurce, At 13, she and her family—she's the oldest of 11 children—moved to a rundown tenement on a mean street in Brooklyn.

She went from the High School of Performing Arts to Harvard University, where she graduated with highest honors, then to Sarah Lawrence College for her master's degree. And last week, Esmeralda Santiago was in Washington, where she was interviewed on public radio, the Voice of America and by TV and newspaper reporters, and gave readings of her just published book, "When I Was Puerto Rican."

Her book is a recollection of those early years, mostly of how the *jibarita* was taken out of the idyllic countryside, but the plantain stain remained.

The title, she explained, is meant to be ironic. When she was growing up in the countryside she had a clear sense of who she was; when she came to the states she was given the amorphous, faceless tag of Hispanic.

"People speak of Hispanics in numbers. To be a Puerto Rican means to be a particular person."

The writing in "When I was Puerto Rican" is shining and clear and beautiful, poetic, comic and moving. Not the least of its accomplishments is that for stateside readers it will show the dignity and the value of a culture that relatively few are aware of here. For Esmeralda Santiago, life in the Puerto Rican countryside may have had its share of poverty and deprivation, but it also was a deeply rich and poignant experience.

Now, 45, the mother of two, owner with her *americano* husband of an educational film production company, she lives in her own home in Westchester County. You look at the demographics, and you see that so many other Puerto Ricans with similar backgrounds never make that kind of breakthrough. You see that Puerto Ricans in the United States, four decades after the main migration, remain the poorest of the poor.

How did Esmeralda Santiago get from Barrio Macún to Harvard University, and beyond?

Her family, she said, are all "very curious people and high achievers." Her five sisters and five brothers have, in their own way, also made it in America. The family did not have the money for medical school for one daughter who wanted to become a doctor, so she became an X-Ray technician. Another is a successful fashion designer. "I was the one who loved to read those big fat books," said Esmeralda Santiago.

But there was something else: "All of us, in one way or another, fulfilled our mother's dream to learn English, to support ourselves, to *desenvolver,* ease ourselves, into the environment."

Esmeralda Santiago became an "American," which for her meant the pain of realizing that she was no longer 100 percent Puerto Rican.

It was painful, she said to have this thrown in her face "time and again" on her trips back to Puerto Rico, as it was painful years before to be "wrenched away against my will, to leave behind what I thought I was growing up to be."

And in the eyes of many Americans, she would, of course, never be 100 percent American.

"So I had to come to terms," she said, "that to Americans I'm Puerto Rican and to Puerto Ricans I'm an American. And now I can function relatively painlessly in both cultures. When I go to Puerto Rico I visit that part of me that is Puerto Rican. It's a constant back-and-forth and I have to choose the proper behavior for each particular situation.

"In order for me to succeed in America I had to buy into things that a lot of people are not willing to buy into. I had to find the balance. People are most successful who balance that toward the American side; you learn English, you learn it well and you play it the way Americans do.

"I call myself a 'hybrid'," she said. "I like that, I think of a beautiful blooming flower.

Santiago mastered English and, in New York, she discovered literature.

"I have to tell you when I discovered Jane Austen my life changed. When I discovered George Eliot my life changed. Others have lived more exciting lives, but I measure my life by my literary experiences. It would have been nice staying a *jibarita*, but maybe I never would have read *Middlemarch*."

Santiago, who last summer "discovered" James Joyce, has become enamored with the great Irish writer and intrigued by the similarities between Irish and Puerto Rican history, each marked by centuries of colonialism and struggles to retain language and culture. She was struck, among other things, by the Joycean creative creed of finding the universal in the particular.

Read her book, you'll see exactly what that means. You will see how one particular woman's journey from a rippled metal shack in a Puerto Rican countryside barrio becomes a story rich in reverberations about all those who have made a transforming physical and spiritual journey in life.

December, 1993

Esmerelda Santiago

Journey into Loisaida

Wassup with the Nuyoricans on the Lower East Side? Well, homegirls are morphing into squirrels and monkeys and seagulls to get around the neighborhood, and occasionally startling an onlooker by fully feathering into magnificent peacocks. The homeboys, who slouch around the projects in baggy clothes by day, are honing in by night on radar, sonar, electronics, navigation and all the other specializations needed for the Puerto Rican Navy being formed to preserve and protect *la isla.*

When the concrete jungle gets the tenement-dwelling Nuyoricans down, those with the magic touch transform their crummy apartments into the enchanted island, where they wade in the warm, emerald-blue waters and relax on the sandy, palm-studded beach of Luquillo, or receive blessings from the Taíno god Yukiyú on the primordial El Yunque mountain top.

Meanwhile, 15-year-old Maruquita Salsipuedes, a juvenile Jennifer López lookalike, falls for punk-rocker Omaha Bigelow, a *simpático* Gringo loser who, unfortunately, is less than well-endowed on the anatomical front. Maruquita calls on her family's *brujería* (witchcraft) background to shape up Bigelow down below.

Omaha is now a big boy with a growing ego. He gives thanks to Maruquita by fulfilling her desire for a "Gringorican" baby—then cheats on her by impregnating four other *Loisaida* ladies. But nobody monkeys with Maruquita, the good witch of the Lower East Side.

Omaha Bigelow, who the 15-year-old Maruquita considers her "pet," gets his comeuppance in terms both figuratively and literally poetic. Read it and weep. Or laugh. Or whatever.

It's all happening in Edgardo Vega Yunqué 's magically realistic, highly raunchy and deeply resonant novel, *The Lamentable Journey of Omaha Bigelow into the Impenetrable Loisaida Jungle,* published by Overlook Press.

And that's not even the half of it. You've got the writer and his characters trading thoughts and opinions on how things are turning out in the novel. The marvelous Maruquita goes from down home Spanglishisms ("What for it gotta be like that?" "Papito, wassup?") when she's in character during the narrative, to sophisticated polisci-speak when she addresses the author in asides about where the novel is going ("is this some sort of metaphysical affirmation of the hegemonic power of the United States juxtaposed against the destiny of the hemisphere?")

You've got the writer commenting in mini-essays on the very unmagical reality of Puerto Rican politics and the plight of the people, and of the sorry state of American life and politics, not to mention the country's fast decaying tastes in literature. The author slices into the heart of conservative America and is on target when he says it often seems that Americans "learn geography by bombing places." (You want fer-instances? How about Kosovo, Fallujah, Samarra, et al.)

The author's poetic imagination swings more than his political prose—he's more profound and gives us deeper insights when he's riffing on the human comedy. And there are intimations of the meaning and/or meaning-lessness of it all, with takes on "Oedipus Rex" to "Waiting for Godot," from Greek god Zeus to, well, Geraldo. And Bill Clinton,

Bush the Younger, the CIA and Vieques also are wrapped into the satirical package.

What you've got is an exceptional American writer of Puerto Rican descent taking chances with both the content and structure of the novel, and bringing most of it home beautifully. Whether you're from Bayamón or the Bronx— and maybe even Omaha, Nebraska—this hilarious and heart-felt novel should hit home with its dark humor and its bittersweet humanity .

April 28, 2005

(The Puerto Rico Rico-born, New York-raised Ed Vega passed away in August, 2008, but his wild and wonderful prose keeps on going on in *Omaha Bigelow,* and in his many other works.)

Edgardo Vega Yunqué

Literature As Sports, Sports As literature

*M*uhammed Ali and Norman Mailer had a mutual friend—World Light Heavyweight Champion José "Chegui" Torres, originally from Ponce, Puerto Rico. That friendship brought both Ali and Mailer to the island as "Chegui" whipped journeyman Tom McNeely at San Juan's Hiram Bithorn Stadium, named after the first Puerto Rican Major Leaguer, who pitched for the Chicago Cubs 1942-1943 and for other teams 1946-1947. Ali fought an exhibition three-rounder before the Torres fight and Mailer attended at ringside. Earlier in the day at the hotel in the tourist section of Condado, where both were staying, Ali and Mailer had decided a good preliminary would consist of what they would bill as the world championship Indian-wrestling match. Fortified by several Bacardi zombies, heavyweight writing contender Mailer battled The Greatest to a draw (observers believed that Ali may have almost thrown the fight), which sent the writer, and several followers, happily back to the hotel bar.

Clay, Mailer in 'Draw'

Novelist Norman Mailer—a bruising stylist in his own field—yesterday held to a draw Heavyweight Champion Cassius "Muhammad Ali" Clay in an under-the-weight, over-the-table, non-championship Indian wrestling match.

The tongue-in-cheek contest took place on the terrace of the San Jeronimo Hilton, where both men are staying. It wasn't clear who challenged whom, but the two locked hands after Clay had good naturedly knocked to the ground a cardboard replica of Light Heavyweight Champion José Torres.

Mailer and the Puerto Rican fighter have become close friends in New York, where they both live. The novelist was in Puerto Rico for the first time to attend last night's fight between Torres and heavyweight Tom McNeeley. Clay also fought an exhibition on last night's card.

Mailer was in good condition after a noontime walk along the beach and two zombie cocktails, but it was not known at presstime whether he considered the former or the latter instrumental in his fine Indian wrestling showing with Clay.

Earlier, Mailer had referred to himself as "the intellectual precursor to Cassius Clay," a reference to the popularity, and in some quarters notoriety, he has received as an individual apart from his typewriter.

In a more serious vein, Mailer made the following comments in an interview:

—The "vitality" of the Puerto Rican people will have a large effect on the United States, providing Puerto Ricans do not get swept up by over-Americanization.

—The best way for an intellectual to deal with modern society is to see how it works. One way he can do this is to "infiltrate" The Establishment, act as a spy and remain true to his ideal of the Renaissance man, who, as an individual, is at war with modern man, destroyer of the ideal.

He is at present working on a new novel, which he says will take many years to complete.

—While there are many good Latin American poets, there are almost no good novelists. Puerto Rico needs a great novelist to portray its social upheaval to the world.

—A novel will generally have more effect as social criticism. than "a work of formal reason."

Expanding his comments on the effects Puerto Ricans and the United States may have on one another, Mailer had this to say:

"If Puerto Ricans absorb and appropriate the culture of America to become larger as people, while still remaining Puerto Rican, they may have a large effect on America. I think the effect of Puerto Ricans, however, still lies in the future.

"What I think America can teach the Spanish soul is that the tragic view of life is possible only when the stakes are high. In Mexico, a man may kill a friend over a drink and be let out of jail long enough to weep at the funeral. Here life is tragic, but the stakes are too small."

Then he added: "Not that we, as Americans, know about the tragic. All we know about is high stakes."

March 11, 1965

Norman Mailer confidently clasps the hand of grimacing World
Heavyweight Champion Muhammed Ali as they hold hands for an
Indian Wrestling Match (*Star* Photo by Marvin W. Schwartz)

Island Education

Church and State have not always had a cordial relationship in Puerto Rico, especially during the reign of Gov. Luis Muñoz Marín (1948-1964); most especially in the election year of 1960, when island bishops urged Catholics to vote against Muñoz. The bishops warned that a vote for Muñoz could actually result that support of his administration could actually result in excommunication, a threat that Francis Cardinal Spellman of New York later said would not happen. The bishops' displeasure with the governor ranged from the administration's campaign against bingo and gambling games for parish fund-raising to the advocacy of family planning and birth control.

Then there were the nuns, who most agree, put good works before policy, as in the case of Sister Anita and her two cohorts, Sister Margaret and Sister Camilus, who spent a good part of their days in 1981 and beyond teaching the children of a poor barrio near Ponce.

The 'Miracle' of Ponce

Ponce, P.R.—It just may be an education "miracle," and it is being performed by three nuns from Brooklyn in the poverty-gripped hills of this south coast city.

The nuns are educating the children of Barrio Tamarindo, where the Caribbean spreads below like a gleaming blue dream but a harsh reality burdens the lives of the people, Most of the 400 families occupy sparsely furnished wooden shacks; only one in 10 of the barrio's inhabitants holds down a steady job; food is cooked over open fires; refrigeration is almost nonexistent.

But the barrio residents take great pride in their school. It offers hope for the future.

Called Central San Francisco, the school was opened in 1975 by Sister Anita Moseley, who came to Puerto Rico 28 years ago from Our Lady of Lourdes Parish in Bedford-Stuyvesant. She is assisted by Sister Margaret Maloney, a Brooklyn native from St. Mary's Parish in Flushing, Queens, and by Sister Camillus Johnston of Good Shepherd Parish in Flatbush.

The nuns belong to the Sisters of St. Joseph Order of Brentwood, L.I. They hold teachers' degrees and are Spanish-speaking. They live in a prefabricated house above the school's third-grade classroom.

The school started as a kindergarten and now goes to the third-grade. A fourth-grade class will begin in August; Sister Anita plans to extend the school to the sixth grade soon after.

Parents are clamoring to get their children into the school.

"They see what our children can do compared to their brothers and sisters in public school," said Sister Anita, who is 66, uses a cane to get around and is tough, outspoken and gutsy. She also enjoys a touching relationship with her pupils, who line up when classes are over for the day to kiss her before leaving.

One student, William Saez, was pronounced unteachable by the public schools, says Sister Anita.

"The only reason they thought he was unteachable," she said, "is because he is so fast and intelligent that as soon as he finished his work, way ahead of the other children, he became like Dennis the Menace. They didn't know how to keep him occupied. We keep him

185

occupied." William has become a top student.

So has eight-year-old Matthieuz de Jesus, who was diagnosed by public health officials as brain-damaged when he was three. Sister Anita took him into her prekindergarten class, where at first he spent the time screaming and jumping around. Today, he is in the third grade and getting straight A's. His IQ has been measured at 134. He reads and understands English well, having picked it up from watching "Sesame Street."

Sister Anita noted that many of her students were in special education classes when they attended public school. "They were told they were stupid. We found out they are normal children." Public schools, she said, give up too quickly on too many poor kids.

Why has central San Francisco succeeded where public schools have failed? "I suppose it's because we live in the barrio and realize the difficulties and give the kids more attention. We know their problems. We have been teaching a long time. I've been at it 43 years. And the other two sisters have been teaching for 35 years. When you're teaching that long, you begin to get what it's about."

An unexpected bonus, said Sister Anita, is the way the children have passed on the school lessons to their parents.

"When I first opened the school," she said, "I had 26 students and about four mothers who could sign their names. Now, I have 130 students and about four mothers who can't write their names. Many of the children are teaching their parents how to read and write."

Parents must dedicate at least two days a month to the tuition-free school. The fathers do construction work, the mothers cook, clean and sew the school uniforms.

"The public school is vandalized, but never this school," said Sister Anita. "The people look after it. Since they are part of it, it is part of them."

The school is run through private donations. Nearby Catholic University provides student teachers and social workers. Sister Anita gets $350 a month from her congregation, Sisters Margaret and Camillus are paid $300 from other sources. The food comes from the school lunch program. Sister Anita has managed to buy six inexpensive micro-computers for the school.

"If you give poor children a poor education they won't get anywhere," said Sister Anita.

"But if you give them an education of excellence, they will progress like any child who gets such an education. God didn't give out brains according to money people have in their pockets."

April 8, 1984

Commemoration

*H*ere is a tribute to a fellow newshound who went
through the 1960s-1980s era at the *Star* and despite his
death in 1992, lives on in words, deeds and spirit.

Courageous, Caring, Consistent

As a journalist, you can learn many tricks of the trade. If you practice enough, you can hone your lead sentence to a bright, clever thing that will make the reader want to read on. You can be alert for that outrageous or salient quote. You can search out those telling details about people and places that vividly set a scene. Given reasonable intelligence and good files, you can give a context to your stories, provide readers with the journalistic "big picture."

But what separates the very good from the very bad and the very ugly in our profession, or trade, or whatever journalism is considered this year, is not taught, and cannot be taught, in any journalism school. It has to do with character and decency and a way of viewing the world, seeing the biggest of big pictures.

Harold Lidin was one of the most consistent journalists, and people, I knew. Consistent in the best sense of that word. His consistency sprung from his character and his decency, and from the way the world appeared before him.

Harold was no saint—God forbid!—though he was probably as close as journalists get. There were times when he was pretty stubborn—especially in those dark years, for me, when I was the *Star's* city editor and had to tell him what to do, and he did what he wanted to do anyway. He had his own agenda, his own "big picture," whether it was interviewing an undersecretary from a small Caribbean island, or passing on the thoughts of a 1930s radical who happened to be in San Juan.

It was his consistency that propelled him to these stories, his view of Puerto Rico as an independent entity, within the context of strong regional ties. Independence was to be achieved on the moral grounds of individual and collective fulfillment. The biggest of big pictures.

Harold was truly absent-minded. He kept losing that Panama hat of his, and Saturdays—the day he worked as a reporter for the *Star* after his alleged retirement—often ended with Harold asking: "Has anyone seen my hat?" What was under that hat, when he wore it, knew how to keep things in place and place things in perspective.

Then there was the other hat. I remember the photo in the *Star* of Harold wearing that World War II Anzac bush hat with the front brim folded back as he was going up some god-forsaken river in Nicaragua with a boatload of *Contras*. Harold Lidin, war correspondent, making a foray into a Central American heart of darkness, probably loving every minute of it, armed with the confidence of his consistency. He sailed through unscathed. A guardian angel always seemed to accompany Harold on his many travels to troubled lands.

Many of the traits I admired in Harold I fell short of myself, and I suppose one of the things that affected me deeply about his death—besides losing a friend—was the passing of that vicarious part of me. Harold was deeply religious. I'm not talking about his daily attendance at Mass; it was not the outer observances of ritual that made him, or makes anyone, religious. It was the *consistency* of his belief. He was against abortion; unlike many so-called religious people, he also opposed capital punishment He believed in the Christian

message of other-worldly justice; he believed in justice in this world, so he supported liberation theology, working people joining together in unions, and the taxing of the rich to help the poor.

He believed "Thou Shalt Not Kill" had no asterisk attached to it that said except in time of war, so he got involved in the *Pax Christi* peace movement and he opposed nuclear weapons at Roosevelt Roads Naval Base.

Objectivity is a word that no longer has much meaning in journalism. Journalists are not recording machines. You bring your life's experiences and your thoughts and ideas to the job and, one way or another, these things find their way into your stories. Since you can never really be objective, you can only try to be fair and honest and knowledgeable and truthful.

Your character often creeps into your stories and certainly informs your columns. It can also produce fine writing. A few Sundays ago Harold and I covered Gov. Hernández Colón's resignation as head of the Popular Democratic Party. Harold was to write about the overall event, and I was to describe the reaction of Sen. Victoria Muñoz Mendoza to the changing of the guard.

The most emotional moment occurred when Muñoz gave the governor a cherished religious medal that was once owned by her father. I described the scene with too much restraint. As sometimes happens when two reporters are sent to the same event, Harold also wrote of that moment.

"In a soft voice that quickly bent under the cross of memory and emotion, Muñoz lauded the governor for his service, then produced a medal she said her father had worn for years. Calling the governor to the microphone, Muñoz pinned the medal on him, and the two melded into the effusive embrace that the audience had been awaiting."

That was a deeply felt, graceful paragraph. It took a person with sensitivity and an understanding of humanity to write it. It took a Harold Lidin.

Feb. 2, 1992

Harold Lidin

Home Again

*I*n 1993, the Friedman family returned to Puerto Rico—as tourists. The following article recounts our experiences in what was once the home where we hung our hearts.

Welcome a Warm One on the Island

For the first time in more than a quarter of a century, I saw Puerto Rico as a tourist—and liked what I saw (mostly).

Even jaded natives would appreciate island essentials after spending a winter like the last one in the states, where it seemed as though hell actually froze over. Never have cloudless skies, a tingling sun, a cooling—but never too cool—sea and rustling breezes seemed so heavenly.

After living 18 months surrounded by the sterile air in and around the nation's capital, one notices the real, live, life-enhancing, nostril-dilating island smells—the warm salt spray by the sea, the frangipani, the spiced cooking in the hallways.

The Friedman family spent the Easter break in your tropical paradise. We spent three days and two nights at *Palmas del Mar* (we got an affordable deal) and six days and nights in an Isla Verde condominium.

Palmas, of course, was other-worldly. It seemed not so much a Caribbean resort as a planned utopian community in a futuristic novel, where everything and everyone is beautific, beautiful and boring. We forwent the tony yacht-crowd waterfront restaurants with *Chez and Casa* in their names for a restaurant high in the Humacao hills named Mr. Nice Place. The *comida* was *criolla* and the price was nice.

The Isla Verde beaches were a pleasant surprise, far different from the reportedly refuse-filled sands of the Condado. The beach behind our condominium, which was next to the Holiday Inn, was fresh-free. And, even on the Easter weekend, it was far from crowded with bathers.

One big complaint, however: The airport runway was right across the road beyond a clump of bushes. The take-offs and landings started at 6:48 a.m., and went on practically non-stop throughout the day. At sunrise, even though lying in bed, you felt that you too were blasting off and earning frequent-flyer miles.

We ate in a variety of Isla Verde restaurants, including one that assured customers it

193

would be open all day on "Holly" Friday. This brought to mind a favorite sign, at the opening of a Mexican restaurant in Hato Rey some years ago, that informed clients the restaurant provided "ballet parking," (Visions of attendants in tights twirling out to meet the vehicles.)

One night, we took the Morocco landscape-like rids along the seaside road into Old San Juan. The palm fronds were ragged shadows against the blue-black sky, which was also etched by domes and cupolas and a minaret like building. My 9-year-old daughter Elizabeth wanted to know what that flashing light show was on the moonlit ocean to our right. It was a cruise ship out of Fellini's *Amarcord,* as brightly lit as a town plaza during a patron saint's festival.

We dined at El Patio de Sam, which seems to have become a shrine to the living legends of the Old City. I boasted to my 13-year-old daughter Madeline that I had been there in the early days, when Sam's was a more modest establishment and the bar gave out to a fully open patio backed by a scruffy gray stucco wall.

Yes, I told Madeline, I had known all those living legends: Carlos Irizarry, whose paintings and prints adorned the restaurant's walls; Edwin Reyes, the poet whose ode to Sam's is printed on placemats on all the tables ("There is a space, a point, a cauldron of energy on San Sebastián Street 108—the coming and going is great in this powerful vortex") and who greeted me from his bar stool at the entrance; George Mabuchi, whose caricatures of old time Sam's regulars (the great Tufino, Bob McCoy, Davey Jones) hang on a back wall.

After dinner, we walked around Plaza Quinto Centenario, packed with people and litter, and watched the kamikaze roller bladers zipping backwards down flights of stairs, wondering what they did for an encore.

We returned the next morning to Old San Juan, because, besides being tourists, we were also on a sentimental journey, and everyone agreed we could not leave Puerto Rico without a breakfast of *mallorcas* and *café con leche* (straight milk for the kids) at *La Bombonera*. On the way, Madeline got misty eyed when she saw a *Pan Pepín* truck and heard the voice of Wally Plerra over WOSO—reminders of the first sweet decade of her life.

Once in *La Bombonera*, my daughters—critiqued the powder-sugared buns, remembering

194

them as larger and more buttery, as they always will be in the *mallorcas* of our dreams.

On the daytime streets of the Old City we exchanged warm embraces with people we vaguely knew and visited the Pigeon Park. Even the kids found it dirty and oppressive, bird droppings and feathers everywhere, especially on the benches, the low cooing of the little beasts enough to drive one up and over the surrounding ancient walls.

But moving around the old streets was still a great pleasure. Lots of stunning views and museums and terrific art—from the Martorell exhibit at the San Juan Museum of Art and History to the more than 100 works from around Latin America at the Colibri Gallery to the Picasso etchings of Ovid's "Metamorphoses" at *La Casa del Libro.*

And, mostly, our pleasure came from the remembrance of things past, the tapping at our hearts when personal nostalgia meshes with the timeless horizons within us all.

April, 1994

Acknowledgements

*M*any thanks to Katie Dahm-Johnson for her patience and editorial skills in helping to get the book in shape.

A thank you to Susan Stern for other technical assistance on photos, etc.

Muchas gracias to Maridale Jackson for proofing the whole works, Spanish and Spanglish included.

Made in United States
North Haven, CT
27 October 2023

43267962R00117